Facing A New Day

Practical help for our times

1 Thessalonians

Dr. Derek Stringer

Good News Broadcasting Association (UK)
Ranskill. DN22 8NN. England
Email:info@gnba.net   Web site:www.gnba.net

Scripture taken from the
HOLY BIBLE NEW INTERNATIONAL VERSIONS
Copyright 1973, 1978, 1984 International Bible Society.
Used by permission of Zondervan. All rights reserved.

British Library Cataloguing In Publication Data

A Record of this Publication is available
from the British Library

ISBN 1846851009
978-1-84685-100-1

Published February 2006 by

Exposure Publishing, an imprint of Diggory Press,
Three Rivers, Minions, Liskeard, Cornwall, PL14 5LE, UK
WWW.DIGGORYPRESS.COM

Contents

Introduction 1Thessalonians

Two church ministers were standing by the side of a road holding up a sign that read, *"The end is near! Turn around now before it's too late!"* A car driver slowed down enough to read the sign and then yelled at the two clergymen, "Leave us alone you religious fruitcakes!" He then sped up and took off down the road. From around the curve, the two ministers heard screeching tires and a splash. One minister looked at his friend with a grin on his face and said, "Do you think we should just make a sign that says, 'The Bridge is out?'"

As we begin a journey through a key book in the Bible, I wonder if some of you are just speeding down the road of life, uncertain about what lies around the corner? At the risk of sounding like a religious nut, for the next few chapters I will be commenting from the book of 1 Thessalonians to help us see that the end is near.

As we come to our study in 1 Thessalonians, it's important to understand why this letter was written.

1. To give instruction about the return of Christ.

Each New Testament book has a special theme or message, that is uniquely its own. Galatians is the freedom letter; Philippians is the joy letter;

and Colossians lifts up the supremacy of Christ. The message of these letters written to the church at Thessalonica is the return of Jesus Christ and how this truth should affect our lives and our churches. Every chapter of 1 Thessalonians concludes with a reference to the end being near.

1:10: *"And to wait for his Son from heaven, whom he raised from the dead-Jesus, who rescues us from the coming wrath."*
2:19: *"For what is our hope, our joy, or the crown in which we will glory in the presence of our Lord Jesus when he comes? Is it not you?"*
3:13: *"May he strengthen your hearts so that you will be blameless and holy in the presence of our God and Father when our Lord Jesus comes with all his holy ones."*
4:17: *"After that, we who are still alive and are left will be caught up together with them in the clouds to meet the Lord in the air. And so we will be with the Lord forever."*
5:23: *"May God himself, the God of peace, sanctify you through and through. May your whole spirit, soul and body be kept blameless at the coming of our Lord Jesus Christ."*

As we walk through this book, we will see that Paul did not look upon the doctrine of Christ's return as a theory to be discussed, but as a truth to be lived.

These letters encourage us to live with an eye on the future, since Jesus is coming when we least expect Him.

2. To give insight to new Christians.

The church at Thessalonica was filled with brand new believers. The apostle Paul started the church but was not able to spend much time teaching them. These letters provide very practical instruction on how to live the Christian life. Some of the topics include conversion, integrity, compassion, the Bible, heavenly rewards, suffering, prayer, moral purity, hard work, the second coming, the role of spiritual leaders, and dealing with difficult people.

3. To inspire hope in the midst of uncertainty.

I define *'hope'* as H.O.P.E. . . *Having Only Positive Expectations.* This young church was in a very dangerous world. The believers were facing persecution and wondered how much more they could take. The parallel to our world is striking. These two letters were written to help believers avoid both withdrawal and hysteria.

Before we jump into 1 Thessalonians, there are several important facts to know about this letter. It's one of the oldest books in the New Testament. It was written less than 20 years after the Resurrection. As such it is one of the earliest pictures we have of the Christian church. If the New Testament had been set out chronologically, instead of starting with the Gospel of Matthew, it would probably have been introduced by 1 and 2 Thessalonians. It was written some years before the Gospel accounts of the earthly ministry of the Lord Jesus Christ. It's one of the shortest books in the New Testament. Everything is simple, clear and direct. If you want to know Paul's doctrine, read Romans. If you want to know his heart, read 1 Thessalonians.

The church at Thessalonica is a model church. If we want to follow an example today, we can look at some successful churches around us, and that can be helpful, but it's even better to try to imitate the faith and love of the Thessalonians. *"And so you became a model to all the believers in Macedonia and Achaia"* (1 Thessalonians 1:7).

That is something worth knowing.

CHAPTER 1
God's Word Is At Work
1 Thessalonians 1:1a

"Paul, Silas and Timothy"

Sir Edward Elgar wrote the following words at the end of the original score of the oratorio 'The Dream of Gerontius' - "This is the best of me; for the rest, I ate and drank and slept and loved and hated, like another; my life was as the vapour and is not; but this I saw and knew; this if anything of mine, is worth your memory". There was the great composer's testimony that his great work meant the world to him. And my purpose in writing is to ask, Can we speak in the same way of our faith? Can we, in an age when subtle forces are striving to undermine the basis of conviction; when specious voices are busy whispering and hinting that the faith we prize is nine-tenths credulity, bad logic, wishful thinking and muddled reasoning; when ethical axioms which once held the field unchallenged are widely repudiated and beliefs which seemed inviolable find themselves fighting for their life and even religious people grow uncertain in their attitude, vague about their witness and excessively problem-conscious? Can we, in such an age, stand up and confront the whole world with the irrefutable assurance of an authentic, first-hand experience and say of our religion, what Elgar said of his music, "This I saw and knew"?

It is important that we should face ourselves with this question. Our religion is going to make no impact whatever on the world. It is going to leave not the slightest impression on the secularism around, *unless* it is our own assured possession. There is nothing contagious about a second-hand faith. If you have a borrowed creed you will never set another person on fire with it. If Christ's people are hesitant and doubtful about fundamentals, from where is the dynamic for an adventuresome Christianity to come?

There are some interesting words of John Ruskin's in 'Modern Painters' that hammer home the point. *"The greatest thing a human soul ever does in this world is to see something and tell what he saw in a plain way. Hundreds of people talk for one who can think, but thousands can think for one who can see. To see clearly is poetry, prophecy and religion – all in one."*

What the world needs today is an army of men and women who, whether they say it with their lips or not, will unmistakably declare it by the light of their eyes, the serenity of their spirits and the decision of their wills: *"This I know and for this I stand! I can't help it. The eyes of my heart have been enlightened."*

If this matter is urgent from the point of view of the impact of our faith upon the world, it is vital also because of the trials, frustrations, disappointments and disasters which our lives are almost bound to meet on their journey through this life. The fact is, the hour may come when everything about you, your very mental health, will depend on precisely the degree to which you have built up, or have failed to build up, an assured and vital faith.

When Paul wrote to the believers in Thessalonica, he could do so with thanksgiving. Paul was accustomed to having his message dismissed by his enemies as man-made, something devised by himself; hence his solemn protest in Galatians 1:11,12: *"the gospel which was preached by me ... is not according to man; for I did not receive it from man nor was I taught it (by man)."* He therefore found it especially encouraging when it was sincerely and spontaneously welcomed as good news from God.

This is crucially important. It means that Christianity is not just another beautiful speculation on the mysteries of life; not a theory of spiritual values, nor a vague mysticism, nor ideas about our ethical duty. It is historical fact. It is the eternal world of spirit intersecting, at a definite point of time and in certain decisive events, this actual world in which we live. It is

God visibly, dramatically and redemptive in action, on the plane of history and amid the hard and often tragic realities of human existence.

Perhaps someone feels – "Some people at Thessalonica may have received the word of God and it worked in their lives: but how can it ever be that for me? I wish I could say the same! I do recognise that for the practical facing of this difficult life, with all its possibilities of trouble and disaster, there can be nothing on earth so steadying and reinforcing as a proved and tested experience of God which is vivid and alive. But how can I get it? There is no point in what you have been saying, unless you can tell me that."

I will tell you now. You can get it precisely as those believers at Thessalonica got it. And how was that? By personal experiment. By the actual process of facing life with Christ. Take any of your spiritual problems – the existence of God, the reality of his provision, the assurance of forgiveness, the power of prayer: in every instance, the experiment of facing life with Christ can transform a vague half-belief into a burning, sure certainty!

The Thessalonian believers became a model to other believers. Their faith in God had become known everywhere (1:8). What their eyes saw, ours, too, may see. What their ear heard, ours too may hear. And we can say, with a conviction," *This is no borrowed, threadbare faith. It is proved experience, my own, my very own!"* If you and I can reach a faith like that, then let the threatening future bring what it may, one thing is certain – we shall not go under! Come night and darkness and crushing blows of discouragement and our feet shall stand upon the rock.

But do remember this: that kind of certainty, that vital first-hand experience of God in Christ, comes only through a great personal venture. You cannot prove that Paul and the church in Thessalonica are right, or share their confident discovery, unless you are ready to risk giving every atom of your personality, body, soul and spirit to Christ's command.

My prayer is that this book will be a source of encouragement, assurance, raw courage and hope for those who long to stand firm in the Lord (3:8).

Now read on and allow me to tell you why.

CHAPTER 2
Frustrations Are Not all Bad
1 Thessalonians 1:1

"Paul, Silas and Timothy, to the church of the Thessalonians in God the Father and the Lord Jesus Christ: Grace and peace to you"

Three couples were discussing words. *" Let me show you something,"* volunteered Vern. He picked up the phone and dialled, *"Hello, is Charlie there?"*

"No," replied a voice, *"and it's gone midnight!!"*

*"That was **irritation,"*** reported Vern.

He dialled the same number *"Hello is Charlie there?"*

They could hear the angry voice at the other end.

*"That was **aggravation."*** said Vern. *"Now I will demonstrate **frustration."*** He dialled the third time and Vern asked, *"Hello, this is Charlie. Have you any calls for me?"*

Frustration can be very trying. No one can make you frustrated. People have an effect on you and situations can be trying, but a state of exasperation is your own doing! You choose your reaction. You probably tell yourself, *"I'm upset."* And the more you reinforce the thought, the more unnerved you feel.

Affirm **"I have frustration."** Don't admit,**" I am a frustrated person."** You *can* separate yourself from the emotion. The emotion is not you. A mood affects you momentarily, but it will pass. **You** are in charge of your thoughts and feelings. **Patience** is one answer to frustration. God is in the business of developing that virtue in those who acknowledge him in all of their ways.

Acts 16:6-11 is Luke's description of a key frustration in the apostle Paul's second missionary journey. Paul, Silas, and the newly recruited Timothy went in search of new converts to Christ in Pamphylia and regions beyond, searching for new frontiers to conquer and were frustrated in the attempt. They were used in ways they could never have planned or anticipated.

Paul wanted to go to the Roman province of Asia, west of Pamphylia extending over the eastern coast of the Aegean Sea. He felt this was God's game plan. However, the Holy Spirit closed the door on the province of Asia. *"Having been kept by the Holy Spirit from preaching the word in the province of Asia."* (Acts 16:6). The Greek word expresses an action prior to entering Asia. The Holy Spirit made it clear that Asia was low priority. We do not know how this was expressed. Perhaps sickness frustrated Paul going. Others have surmised that resistance from the Jews made the journey indefensible. Still others have supposed direct, inner guidance from the Holy Spirit to the mind of Paul. Whether the Holy Spirit said *"No"* in inner feelings or outer frustrations, the result was the same; Paul was stopped before he started out for Asia.

With Asia's door slammed shut by the Holy Spirit, Paul led his team north to preach throughout Phrygian and Galatian territory. Unanticipated frustrations occurred all along the way. People discovered new life in the Lord Jesus Christ and churches were born. Paul's letter to the Galatians hints at the extent of this phase of the mission.   But the greatest adventure in the gospel is still ahead. Further north, the team approached the border of Mysia. *"They tried to enter Bithynia, but the Spirit of Jesus would not allow them to." (*Acts 16:7). Here the Greek verb is a present active form, which means that, whereas the first prohibition was prior, this one was concurrent. Paul and his team wanted to go in one direction. The Lord wanted them to go in the opposite direction. Another door closed, so they travelled east to Troas on the Aegean coast.

Remember, frustrations can be the means of disappointing to re-appoint. *'During the night Paul had a vision of a man of Macedonia standing and begging him, "Come over to Macedonia and help us."'* (Acts 16:9). Now Paul knew the uncertain 'holding pattern' was over. Here was a clear direction. The team will preach the gospel in Macedonia. The Acts account becomes first person at this point. This is the first of the "we" passages, announcing that it was at Troas that Luke himself joined Paul and his team. The term Luke uses to describe the essence of the Lord's guidance indicates that perhaps intellect and revelation had combined to make the direction unquestionably clear. *"After Paul had seen the vision, we got ready at once to leave for Macedonia, concluding that God had called us to preach the gospel to them."* (Acts 16:10). The word "conclude" means "to go together, to make things agree and arrive at a conclusion". That strongly suggests that the vision confirmed what God was saying to each of them. He had brought them together in this seaport. Questions like these must have been asked: *"Lord what are you trying to tell us? Why the shut doors? What next? Where do you want us to go according to your limitless wisdom and plan? Macedonia?"* The vision removed all doubts. The focus of the Church was fundamentally changed and incalculably released to transform the world. Europe and eventually the world mission of the Church resulted from the frustration at Mysia. G. Campbell Morgan affirms: *"It is better to go to*

Troas with God than anywhere else without him." Because Paul went to Troas with God, he could now bring God's good news to Europe. What a wonderful frustration to his original plans! The Lord's **"No"** becomes part of His ultimate **"Yes."**

As we acknowledge our Lord in all our ways, we can depend on both reason and our inner feelings. If we have surrendered all to him, we can dare to trust both our adverse and affirmative thoughts and feelings. There are possibilities which are not God's maximum for us if we are open to what he has planned. It was not the Lord's timing for Paul to go into Asia, although later it would be right for him to go to Ephesus on the coast of that province. The Lycus valley of the region would never be personally reached by Paul. Colossae, Laodicea and the other cities of the area would be reached later by his disciple Epaphras and would be charged by the Lord to the ardent care of the Apostle John. God gave his **"No"** about going into Asia at that time because he wanted to get him on to Macedonia. With hindsight, we can see that he was right.

We all know times when we feel hindered and certain directions seem to be wrong. I am awed by all the good, appealing things I have almost done in my life. Looking back, they would have been calamitous for the supreme things God wanted me to do. I have heard the indisputable **"No"** when I determine not to do what seemed so right by my own standards of appraisement, I turn to see a new outlook. But going in the direction, in which one is guided, always involves hazard. Paul and his team pressed on, taking the risk, for the Holy Spirit knew what He was doing with them. They did not decline to advance when at any point they were prohibited by the Spirit from going into Asia or Mysia; they risked moving in new directions each time. The way they had chosen was disqualified by the Lord. This got them to Troas and gave them an assurance of what they were to do.

There are times I wish the Lord would write out the instructions *(in triplicate and confirmed by fax)* and send them by angelic messenger *(preferably an arch-angel)* so that I would know what I am to do and say on every point for the rest of my life. But the Lord knows me too well to do that! He knows that I would put my trust in the teachings and not in regular daily, contact with him. He gives me the long-range goals, certainly. I am not at all hesitant about the focal aim of my life to proclaim the gospel and be part of his Church. But for the daily decisions about precedence, he gives only as much as I need to know in order to do his will in each situation. The venture is in daring to believe that he will be resolute to give me all I need to know, say and do in the fleeting challenge or opportunity. That way I can learn from both the failures and successes. When I give the Holy Spirit a willing and open mind, alert and aware sensibility and live in constant communication, he does give me clear-sightedness, although along the road there will be surprises I never visualised. Our confidence is that God knows what he is doing; he can get through to us with his intention; our willingness makes possible this phenomena; and he will use our obedience as occasions of growth we never imagined possible.

Paul, Silas, Luke and Timothy arrived first in Philippi where they led Lydia and her household to Christ and there established a church. (Acts 16:11-40) Paul and Silas were arrested on false charges, beaten and put into prison. God delivered them and they were able to lead the jailer and his household to faith in Christ. After encouraging the new believers, Paul and his friends left Philippi (though Luke probably stayed behind temporarily) and headed 100 miles S.W. for the important city of Thessalonica. The synagogue gave them a natural bridge for communicating the gospel. *"Some of the Jews were persuaded and joined Paul and Silas, as did a large number of God-fearing Greeks and not a few prominent women."* (Acts 17:4)

And so the church was born in Thessalonica.

You can visit Thessalonica today, only the travel brochure will call it Thessaloniki. (It used to be known as Salonika). It is an important industrial and commercial city in modern Greece and is second to Athens in population. The Jews of the city became so enraged by his teaching about Jesus that they created a riot and took captive Paul's host, Jason, holding him responsible for the apostle's behaviour.

From Luke's record it may appear that Paul and Silas left the city almost as soon as they arrived (Acts 17:10). I don't think so! There is ample evidence for Paul's letter to the Thessalonians that a lot of time elapsed between verses 4 and 5 in Acts 17. The team probably spent some months ministering to new believers and winning others for Christ. Paul gave in-depth teaching that would have taken a lengthy period of time (1 Thessalonians. 2:7-10). Paul left the city, travelling south to Berea and there began to preach again. The Jews from Thessalonica, however, followed him, creating another uprising in Berea. Finally, Paul was sent on alone to Athens. He remained but a short time there and he addressed this letter to the new believers in Thessalonica. Paul is clearly the real author of the letter (cf. 2:18; 3:5; 5:27). But Silas and Timothy share his concern for the Thessalonians' spiritual growth. Silas was a member of the Jerusalem church and a Roman citizen. He replaced Barnabas as Paul's colleague on the second missionary journey (Acts 15:40). Silas was content to play second fiddle. How unlike some people. If they can't be number one they refuse to be anything else. An opportunity to be the first violin of the London Philharmonic is turned down in preference to being captain of the Titanic. Not so with Silas.

It's never easy to take a subordinate position to a person of outstanding ability and strong personality. But one characteristic of a Christian servant is his readiness for unnoticeable service in places of secondary significance.

Timothy may still have been a teenager, perhaps 19. He joined Paul (perhaps 50 years old) at Lystra and was to become the apostle's most trusted lieutenant (Acts 16:1). When the town fathers at Thessalonica demanded Jason's guarantee that Paul's team would leave the city, they travelled to Berea, 50 miles away. More trouble stirred up the people against the missionaries, so the believers sent Paul to Athens while Timothy and Silas stayed at Berea. Paul soon sent for Timothy to join him at Athens. (Acts 17:10-15). At this time Timothy received his first solo assignment. He had been with Paul just a year or so and would have been only 20 or 21. Paul sent Timothy back to Thessalonica to strengthen and encourage the faith of the new believers. William Barclay compares Timothy to a postage stamp: "The postage stamp sticks to its job. It is stuck on the envelope and there it stays until it has reached its destination... It did not matter to Timothy where he was sent. He went. It was enough for him that Paul wanted him to go... One of the great tests of any person is if he can really put his back into the things that he does not want to do." (*God's Young Church, Westminster*).

Timothy, Paul's understudy, had passed a major test as a trainee in his visit to Thessalonica.

Don't miss the double address Paul has for the church, one geographical, the other spiritual. They lived in Thessalonica but they were also found *"in God the Father and the Lord Jesus Christ"* This address is the more important of the two. If we have come to Christ we must see ourselves as primarily new creatures *"in the Lord Jesus Christ"* and *"in God the Father."* The apostle will stress this truth throughout this letter.

As usual Paul's prayer for his readers is that they may be blessed with the grace that brings peace and prosperity to the whole man. "Grace is the love of God, spontaneous, beautiful, unearned, at work in Jesus Christ for the salvation of sinful men; peace is the effect and fruit in man of the reception of grace*." (James Denny, The Epistle of the Thessalonians, Hodder & Stoughton).*

So the letter begins. The frustrations of ministry, the strategies and plans discarded. The questioning heart, "What do we do now, Lord?" Guidance is not something we go to God to receive. It is the inner assurance, which comes from being carried along in the stream of the Holy Spirit, through the rocks and rapids of dangerous alternatives. Paul and his team were being carried by the river of the Holy Spirit. They were not so much seeking guidance as in the flow of guidance. Each decision was not an occasion to reintroduce themselves to the Spirit;

rather they were swept along, given instructions and directions before and in the midst of each phase of the evolving mission. Frustration? Yes! But also surprises we never anticipated. The Gospel in Europe.

Christian ministry is going where you're sent: staying where you're put, doing as you're told, repeating what you're told and leaving when you're done. To be 'sent' means that someone else initiates their activity in your life. Someone else is responsible for that which they have initiated. Our efficiency without God's sufficiency leads to deficiency.

Let's learn from the up-and-down life 'happenings' of Paul and his team.

Being a Christian does not always make life easy. In some ways it does. After all, Jesus said, "My yoke is easy and my burden is light." (Matthew 11:30). Jesus promised, "I am with you always, to the very end of the age." (Matthew 28:20). God has said, "Never will I leave you; never will I forsake you." (Hebrews 13:5). I have had people share with me their great disappointment with God because they thought he promised them better than they got in life. When they became followers of Jesus they understood that he would answer all their

prayers, solve all their problems, heal all their diseases and make life constantly happy. Then came sickness, sadness and setbacks that really

24

hurt and took them by surprise. It is not what they thought the Christian life would be like. We must beware of the idea that the Christian life is always easy. It is not. The Christian life is good. The Christian life is supernatural. The Christian life is special. But it is not easy.

"No temptation has seized you except what is common to man" (1 Cor.10:13). There are troubles in life that are part of the universal human experience. It is part of living in our world and no one is exempt. Christians are as vulnerable to natural disasters, mental illness, financial losses and family problems as anyone else. Please don't think that because of faith in Jesus Christ as Saviour we are immunised against life. The difference is not what happens to us but how we respond to what happens. Don't get discouraged! It can be tough to be a Christian. We don't want tough times but we should not be surprised by them. On the contrary, we should consider it a privilege to belong to Jesus Christ whether life is easy or hard.

In 1914 Ernest Shackleton sailed from England with a 27-member crew aboard the *Endurance* headed for the largely unexplored continent of Antarctica. His biographers tell about an ad he ran in a London newspaper in anticipation of his journey:
"MEN WANTED FOR HAZARDOUS JOURNEY. LOW WAGES, BITTER COLD, LONG HOURS OF COMPLETE DARKNESS. SAFE RETURN

DOUBTFUL. HONOUR AND RECOGNITION EVENT OF SUCCESS." 5,000 men volunteered to go.

Far more than signing up with Shackleton, becoming a Christian is joining a great adventure with God. It is exhilarating, promising and spectacular but there are inevitable frustrations along the way and billions have volunteered. The Christian life is very good but don't be surprised when it is also very hard. *"Dear friends, do not be surprised at the painful trial you are suffering, as though something strange were happening to you."* (1 Peter 4:12) Recognising the difficulties of life God promises special provisions for followers of Jesus. *"Do not lose heart. Though outwardly we are wasting away, yet inwardly we are being renewed day by day. For our light and momentary troubles are achieving for us an eternal glory that far outweighs them all. So we fix our eyes not on what is seen, but on what is unseen. For what is seen is temporary, but what is unseen is eternal"* (2 Corinthians 4:16-18). The point Paul is making is that the troubles and delays of life are temporary; they will pass and Christians will experience the wonder of heaven when today's troubles will be forgotten.

As Christians our lives are not always easy. We experience the same universal problems of life as everyone else. We may even suffer extra pain and problems just because we are followers of Jesus. But when we do, God steps in and provides supernatural love, care, promise and strength. We get to experience God in new and deeper ways because of the problems of life. It is not that Christians have a life that is easier but that we have a God who is greater!

In December 1914 the Endurance entered the ice fields of the Weddell Sea. The pack ice froze around them and the promises of the ad started to come true: "HAZARDOUS JOURNEY. LOW WAGES, BITTER COLD, LONG HOURS OF COMPLETE DARKNESS. SAFE RETURN DOUBTFUL." They stayed in and around the ice-locked ship for ten months. No one else in the world knew they were there. Finally the ice crushed the ship. Twenty-eight men started walking across the frozen sea, dragging three lifeboats and minimal supplies. When they reached open water they floated to Elephant Island. It seemed hopeless. Between them and South America was the Drake Passage with the roughest seas in the world. Shackleton and four crewmembers took one of the lifeboats and headed away from South America toward South Georgia Island where there was a whaling station. Without adequate navigation equipment they aimed for a speck in the Southern Atlantic Ocean that was 800 miles away. Bitter cold and dangerous waters surrounded them. They were the only hope for the 23 men left behind on Elephant Island. Shackleton was a committed Christian. He prayed for God's grace and God got them to South Georgia Island. But they landed on the wrong side. The whaling station was on the other side of a mountain range that had never been climbed by humans. Without experience or proper climbing equipment, Shackleton and two of his men headed up the mountains and over ice fields, through blizzards and over treacherous cliffs. They made it in 36 hours. Ernest Shackleton wrote in his diary:

"I know that during that long and racking march of 36 hours over the unnamed mountains of South Georgia, it seemed to me often that there were four, not three. I said nothing to my companions, but afterwards Worsley said to me, 'Boss, I had a curious feeling that there was another person with us".

God did not preserve them from difficulty but he climbed their mountains by their sides. They reached the whaling station. They led the whalers back to the Antarctic Peninsula and Elephant Island where the other twenty-three crewmembers were marooned and rescued them all. Not one was lost.

God has not promised us a life of ease. He has promised us himself and grace sufficient for whatever we face.

CHAPTER 3
Growing Up Or Settling Down?
1 Thessalonians 1: 2-10

"We always thank God for all of you, mentioning you in our prayers. We continually remember before our God and Father your work produced by faith, your labour prompted by love and your endurance inspired by hope in our Lord Jesus Christ. For we know, brothers loved by God, that he has chosen you, because our gospel came to you not simply with words, but also with power, with the Holy Spirit and with deep conviction. You know how we lived among you for your sake. You became imitators of us and of the Lord; in spite of severe suffering, you welcomed the message with the joy given by the Holy Spirit. And so you became a model to all the believers in Macedonia and Achaia. The Lord's message rang out from you not only in Macedonia and Achaia—your faith in God has become known everywhere. Therefore we do not need to say anything about it, for they themselves report what kind of reception you gave us. They tell how you turned to God from idols to serve the living and true God and to wait for his Son from heaven, whom he raised from the dead—Jesus, who rescues us from the coming wrath".

"School days are the best days of your life." some people say. I don't agree. I looked forward to the time when mine came to an end, even though I was an *outstanding* pupil. *'Outstanding'* in the corridor, and *'outstanding'* in the front of the Head Teacher's office. I detested most the end of term reports. I required a signature from a parent acknowledging the report. At least I didn't have the indignity of a boy in one school. The physical growth of the boys was recorded and one boy was 5ft 4inch at the beginning of school term and 5ft 1inch at the end. The schoolteacher, not at all perturbed, wrote on his report, "settling down nicely". This is funny when it comes to a school report, tragic when it comes to a Christian life. We are meant to *"grow in the grace and knowledge of our Lord and Saviour Jesus Christ".* (2 Peter 3:18).

Paul needed to leave Thessalonica in a hurry, possibly after only a few months. But he left a growing Church and he always remembered them in his prayers, thanking God for all of them.

QUESTION: How far forward are we in our Christian growth?

Have we developed over the last six months? As we consider the rapid growth at Thessalonica we can evaluate our growth pattern.

What is the sign of growth?

It is not the number of people who attend church services, but the presence of three qualities. FAITH, LOVE, HOPE. In the New Testament, these are always listed as fundamental characteristics of those who have come to Christ. (Cf. Ephesians 1:15-16,18; Colossians 1:3-5; 2 Thessalonians. 1:3; Philippians. 1:4-5). FAITH roots us in the past and the history of Calvary. LOVE roots us in the present of our walk with God and relating to one another. HOPE takes us into the future. It is more than the wishful thinking of the kettle. Up to its neck in hot water but keeps on singing. Christian hope is firm and established.

These three are actions not attitudes." *Work* produced by faith, your *labour* prompted by love and *endurance* inspired by hope" (v.3).

Have we *faith* that acts?

Faith that doesn't act is not faith at all. A prayer meeting was being held in an area of terrible drought. The people came to pray for rain. Just one girl brought an umbrella. Faith put into practice is the kind of faith by which growth is measured; people who are not operating from their own resources but being stretched. It has been said, "We are not saved by faith plus works, but by faith that works." Check your growth. Have you a developing, growing faith?

Not a naiveté but trusting God for what may seem impossible.

Have we got a *love* that labours?

More is said in the New Testament about love than
any other quality. We use the word love so generally. I love my wife. I love my dog. I love strawberries and cream. Is love measured primarily by how we feel? No! It is what we do, not how we feel. Of course we can feel affection and God can give us affection for others that we naturally would not have. But love is more than that. *"We always thank God for a love that made you work hard,"* says Paul.

Have we a *hope* that hangs in?

"Endurance inspired by hope in our Lord Jesus Christ" (v.3). There is faith, love and plenty of hope in this world, but the Lord Jesus Christ does not inspire it and it will not last. Hope provides patience. We are able to take a long view of things. The shortness of history and the length of eternity give us patience with the baubles of life.

QUESTION: what is the source of this growth?

Verses 4-8 simply give three sources of growth. PREDESTINATION, PREACHING, PRACTICE.

Predestination - *"Brothers loved by God we know that he has chosen you"* (v.4). God does not do anything unless he decides to do it. The Christian life does not begin with man's decision but with God's decision for us. God does not create provisions to meet our problems. He allows problems to meet his provisions. When God created the world, Adam did not have to hold his breath until God could create some air to breathe. God provided the supply before there was a need.

Which came first, the last Adam (Jesus Christ) or the first Adam? The *last* Adam. Which came first, sin or salvation? Paul tells us we were chosen in Christ *before* the foundation of the world (Ephesians 1:4; Revelation 13:8). Before there was a garden in Eden there was a cross on Calvary. God had already taken the initiative. Salvation was always in the heart of God. It was not an afterthought. He believed it was worth the risk to have an extended family for his Son Jesus Christ, in what would eventually be a new earth and a new heaven. There is no need in your life which God has not already met. *"He has blessed us in the heavenly realms with every spiritual blessing in Christ"* (Ephesians1:3). We do not have to pray, like the little girl, "Our Father who art in heaven, how do you know my name."

We do not have to sing:

"To those of us who know the pain,
Of Valentines' that never came.

33

And those whose names were never called,
When choosing sides for Basketball."

We usually think of hypocrisy as someone projecting an image of being better than they actually are. However, it is as much hypocrisy to project an image of being worse than you are actually are! "We are God's workmanship created in Christ Jesus to do good works, which God prepared in advance for us to do" (Ephesians 2:10). Literally, His work of art. We are unique. No one has ever been made just like us. Therefore, we can offer to God something that no one else ever can.

A Tattoo Shop in Hong Kong has a standard tattoo on offer (at a discount price) 'Born To Lose'. Asked if anyone actually wants that tattoo, the answer given by the shop owner is, "Oh yes. But before tattoo on skin – tattoo on mind." Too many people have a loser attitude. "His divine power has given us everything we need for life and godliness through our knowledge of him who called us by his own glory and goodness" (2 Peter 1:3). I think that our lives will be well on the way to being transformed if we would begin each day, for thirty day, saying that out loud and asking God to help us to really believe it. There are, after all, two ways to start the day. You can begin by saying, 'Good morning Lord' or 'Good Lord, it's morning. Begin the day reminding your self of the kind of God He is. All that we need, we have already. It is a matter of appropriating what we have.

Every time we pray we recognise we cannot make people believe in Jesus Christ. All we can do is move them in that direction and remove some of the darkness from their thinking. When we pray, we look for the moving of a sovereign God, who by his Spirit can illuminate their thinking and start the process that will bring them life. It is God who takes the initiative and it is his love that decides those whom he will call. This is not arbitrary.

We know *why* God chooses. He loves to choose nobodies. If we want to see God at work look around for nobodies. God loves to seek and save that which is lost.

We know *how* God chooses. It was the Holy Spirit who told Paul to go to Thessalonica. "We know that God has chosen you because our Gospel came to you not simply with words, but also with power, with the Holy Spirit and deep conviction" (v 4,5).

I can preach my heart out, try to be persuasive, reasonable, logical and technical for the appropriate people and nothing will happen. God must set the ball rolling. We don't know who God will next convert. Who would have thought that Paul the former Saul of Tarsus, whilst breathing out threats against Christians, would have been called of God. Paul writing to the Galatians said that God "set me apart from birth", (Galatians 1:15).

God chose the main means to bring this about.

PREACHING - One of my worries today is the drop in morale about preaching. Parents can unwittingly hinder the spiritual growth of their children by saying. "Now this is going to be an adult sermon, you will not get anything out of it." Who says so? History testifies that God can take something preached and apply it deeply into the lives of boys and girls. Murray McCheyne, greatly used by the Lord in spiritual revival, tells of children coming together for prayer meetings, little boys and girls becoming evangelists. As they grew up physically, they also grew spiritually.

The revered Bible commentator Matthew Henry was converted at the age of eleven. The greatly used American theologian and scholar Jonathan Edwards was aged eight. Puritan Pastor Richard Baxter was six years old. Youth does not give God our ability but our availability.

Let us get rid of phrases like "Stop preaching at me." Find another expression. Recognise the importance of presenting God's truth to people.

Two Scottish ministers were lamenting the good congregation on a Sunday morning, but a dismal one on Sunday evening. People would turn out in the morning but would not come back for Bible study on a Sunday evening. One minister commented that he had tried everything. He had even invited the local football team and the town band but the congregation did not come. Three months later he decided to close the Sunday evening service. The other minister asked, "What did your Elders say about that?" The minister replied. "They don't know I have closed it yet."

Other things are helpful but it is preaching that God uses. God has ruled out man's wisdom as a way of getting to heaven, otherwise it would be salvation by works. When God's word is proclaimed works are completely ruled out. Preaching is something we all can do. We can gossip the Gospel. But it is a certain kind of preaching which will be effective.

A story is told by Dr. Mahaffy, former provost of Trinity College Dublin. When asked by a local clergyman how he had liked his sermon, Dr. Mahaffy replied: "It was like the peace and mercy of God." The clergyman was deeply flattered and wanted to know why he was making such a sublime comparison. " Well," said Dr. Mahaffy, " it was like the *peace* of God because it passed all understanding and like his *mercy* because it showed every sign of enduring for ever." *(Murray Watts, Hot under the Collar, Monarch Publications).*

Question: Why did the psalmist prefer to be a doorkeeper in the house of the Lord?

Answer: So he could stay outside while the sermon was being preached.

Some preachers don't need to put more fire in their sermons; they need to put more sermons in the fire. Paul was not an impressive orator. He didn't have an attractive way of presenting things. Legend suggests that he was bow-legged, balding and small in stature.

George Whitfield, mightily used by God had a squint. Christmas Evans, a great-anointed evangelist, had a false eye. Twenty minutes into his sermon his eye socket would fill up with moisture. He would take out the false eye, wipe the socket with a handkerchief and pop the false eye back again.

God mightily used that man. He continually uses many people whose presentation would definitely not make them television personalities with the correct sound bytes. The Word of God is never out of date; it is always relevant. A man can be thoroughly sound and send his congregation sound asleep *if* the power of the Spirit is missing.

R T Kendal, past minister of Westminster Chapel tells a story (against himself) of memorising and preaching Jonathan Edwards famous sermon, 'Sinners in the hands of an angry God'. When Edwards delivered that address five hundred strong men were hanging onto church pillars and women were fainting. It began the great evangelical awakening. R T Kendal preached it. His congregation yawned. Some years later he was encouraged when he discovered that

Jonathan Edwards himself, repeated that sermon and also had no impact.

"Our Gospel came to you not simply in words but also with power and with the Holy Spirit and with deep conviction." (v.5). If we are not convicted or don't practise what we preach, we will not be able to convince anybody else and our preaching will fall to the ground.

PRACTICE - "You know how we lived among you for your sake. You became imitators of us and of the Lord" (v.5,6). Most things we learn are by imitation. Watch a little girl playing with her dolls imitating her mother. Watch a boy in his toy car manoeuvring so adeptly between the gateposts imitating his dad. Watch him turning backwards on two wheels screeching and bumping the lamppost – imitating his mother!

The Thessalonians imitated the evangelistic team. Despite severe suffering, they welcomed with joy the message given by the Holy Spirit. They became a model to all the believers. This tribute is high praise. Why? Because Paul gave this distinction to no other church.

"The communication of the Gospel is by seeing as well as hearing. This double strand runs through the entire Bible: image and word; vision and voice; opening the eyes of the blind; unstopping the ears of the deaf. Jesus is the Word of God. Jesus is the image of God. The Word became visible; the image became audible. Now the verbal element in evangelism is clear. Where is the visual? And the answer is: in Gospel churches, communities that are changed by the power of the Gospel." *(John Stott quoting Canon Douglas Webster, The Gospel, The Spirit, The Church. S.T.L.1978).*

"A poor widow in Guatemala was down to her last twenty cents and without food. She began to pray about her problem. As she was praying, she felt a deep conviction that God was telling her to go to the large supermarket in town the next day and fill up several carts with groceries and take them to checkout stand number 7. This was not just a vague feeling on her part but a deep, Spirit-born conviction. She went to the supermarket the next morning, loaded enough groceries into carts to last two or three months and took them to checkout 7. Just as she got there the cashier closed the stand to go out to lunch. She suggested that the woman, take her groceries to another stand, but the woman said, "No, I cannot. My Father told me to take these through checkout stand 7." So she waited while the clerk went to lunch and came back again. The clerk was surprised to see the woman still there and started to check out her groceries. Just then an announcement came over the loudspeaker: "This is our seventh year of business and we are pleased to announce that whoever is checking out at checkout stand number 7 gets free groceries!"

Now I am not telling you to do what this woman did. What I am saying is that we are to believe that God cares for us, that he is a loving Heavenly Father and he has a thousand and one ways of meeting our needs but he hardly ever does the same thing twice"! *(Ray Stedman, Discovery Papers 1978).*

The Thessalonians demonstrated a practical faith. The message rang out around Greece and was known everywhere. The imitators were now the imitated! There was nothing left for the team to do. They could move on because those who had come to faith were gossiping the message. The commission to make disciples is not to the church, it is to the individual.

What will we do about our personal responsibility? Are we going for growth? The **signs** are *faith, love* and *hope.* The **source** is *predestination, preaching* and *practice.*

WHERE DO WE START?

Paul uses three verbs to show us three **steps** to take. *Turn, serve* and *wait.*

"You turned to God from idols to serve the living and true God and to wait for his Son from Heaven." (v.9-10). The moment we *turn* to God we are expressing faith. When we *serve* the Lord we express love. As we *wait* for the coming of the Lord Jesus we are expressing hope.

41

TURN TO GOD

The word for "turned" in the Greek is the same word used for conversion throughout the New Testament. God cannot be seen if we have our backs to him. We cannot hear him if we are walking away from him.

Notice the direction of this action: to God from idols. It is not put the other way around. You do not leave your idols for some reason and then painfully try to find God. What happens is that you discover something of the beauty and greatness of God and seeing that and wanting it, you are willing to forsake the cheap and gaudy things with which you have been trying to satisfy yourselves.

Read this carefully. We tend to think that we have to clean ourselves up first, and then, after we have become more spiritually presentable, then we will get serious about our faith. We have it backwards. We cannot get straightened out ourselves on our own. The issue is not improving our behaviour. It is turning to God. Clean up times come later. "We maintain that a man is justified by faith apart from observing the law" (Romans 3:28). The order Is significant. We cannot leave our idols and then try to find God. What happens is that we discover the goodness and greatness of God as we see the changed lives of His followers. When we see it, we want it, and so we turn to God.

We may not bow down to a lump of wood, but whatever has the first place in our lives, is our idol. Some parents idolise their children, some idolise the car. Many of us would label television as an idol. I do not think so. It is rather, an altar upon which are spread offerings and sacrifices to the great god of self. Television panders to our desire for comfort and amusement. It lures us to think always of our own comfort, our pleasure, and our fear of tedium or desire to be either enthused or frightened by watching some display or event. It encourages us to focus upon ourselves.

Our growth will begin when we turn "to God from idols to serve the living and true God" (v.9). The word 'serve' is the same word used for a slave. It is in the present tense to show that service is a continual activity, not a once-in-awhile action. Serving is a lifestyle.

SAVED TO SERVE

Do you feel worthless, untalented or too old? You are still breathing aren't you? If you are unsure go to the bathroom mirror and breathe on it. If a thin mist is left, you are still alive. There is something you can do. As a young Pastor with my 'L' plates on, I was often very direct in some of the things I would say. I would now be just as direct but I would clothe my words. On one occasion, I asked a man if he would be willing to help in a youth club. The man whimpered, "I'd love to help, but I'm so worthless and undeserving." Before I could stop myself I said, "Off course you are! If we had anybody superior, do you think we'd ask you?" That was hardly a tactful or Christian remark, but I am sure there are innumerable pastors who feel like doing the same thing when they face similar occurrences.

God can use imperfect persons to do his perfect will. Our service is dependent upon what God is, not what we are. Serving others is the way to achieve joy and fulfilment, as you learn to encounter God through those people whom you serve.

There is a true story of a boy who suffered under the Nazis during World War II that clearly communicates what I am trying to put into words.

"A Jewish boy was living in a small Polish village when he and all the other Jews of the vicinity were rounded up by the Nazi SS Troops and sentenced to death. This boy joined his neighbours in digging a shallow ditch for their graves. Then they were lined up against a wall and machine-gunned. Their corpses fell into the shallow grave and then the Nazis covered their crumpled bodies with dirt. But none of the bullets hit this little boy. His naked body was splattered with the blood of his parents and when they fell into the ditch, he pretended to be dead and fell on top of them. The grave was so shallow that the thin covering of dirt did not prevent air from getting through to him so that he could breathe. Several hours later, when darkness fell, this ten-year-old boy clawed his way out of the grave. With blood and dirt caked to his little body, he made his way to the nearest house and begged for help. Recognising him as one of the Jewish boys marked for death by the SS, the woman who answered screamed at him to go away and slammed the door. He was turned away at the next house as well as at the one after that. In each case, the unwillingness to risk getting into trouble with the SS troops overpowered any feeling of compassion that these people might have had. Dirty, bloodied, and shivering, the little boy limped from one house to the next begging for somebody to help him. Then something inside seemed to guide him to say something that was very strange for a Jewish boy to say. When the next family responded to his timid knocking in the still of the night, they hear him cry, "Don't you recognise me? I am the Jesus you say you love."

After a poignant pause that must have seemed like an eternity to the little boy, the woman who stood in the doorway swept him into her arms and kissed him. From that day on, the members of that family cared for that boy as though he was one of their own." *(Tony Campolo, Who Switched the Price Tags, Word Books 1986).*

The woman who took him in on that horrible night told this story. She told the story not to elicit praise for herself, but to tell others of the joy and happiness he had brought to her over the years. She had discovered that labouring to help hurting people is serving Jesus Himself. What could be more fulfilling work than that?

Have you turned to the living God? Are you serving other people for him?

WHAT ARE YOU WAITING FOR?

"Wait for his Son from heaven, whom he raised from the dead – Jesus, who rescues us from the coming wrath." (v.10). The word for "wait" occurs only here in the New Testament. It implies maintained expectancy.

An interesting feature about the Thessalonian letters is that each chapter of both letters ends with a reference to the coming of the Lord. At Christmas we look back to his first coming, but in the early church there was little mention of that. They celebrated it. But for them, they believed that he was coming again and their hope lay in that. It was the ever-present hope of the early church and hope became the ascendant theme of these Thessalonians letters. They looked backward to the resurrection. That fact was their answer to the threat of personal death. This was their ground of confidence for conquest over death. Jesus had said, "Because I live you shall live also."

I believe the Scriptures teach that every believer at his or her death is caught up in the return of Christ: that then, for each of us, we become part of the great eternal event, which later will come rushing into time. When is Christ coming? The answer is that he is no further away than your own death. You may not be here tomorrow. If that is so, for you Christ has come; the return of Christ is accomplished. Jesus promised, "If I go and prepare a place for you, I will come back and take you to be with me that you also may be where I am" (John 14:3). What a wonderful promise. We can look back to the resurrection, where we see our victory over death assured. We can look forward to a time that Paul calls "the coming wrath". That is not hell. He is not talking about the fact that Christians are delivered from the fires of hell. John 5:24 records the words of Jesus, "Whoever hears my word and believes him who sent me has eternal life and will not be condemned; he has crossed over from death to life."

The Thessalonians knew they had already learned from Paul that they would not come into that judgement. But here he is talking about a coming wrath. The use of the present tense indicates that it is something yet future. Jesus would also rescue them from that wrath.

In the Old Testament this period is called "the terrible day of the Lord". It is a time when God's judgement will come down upon the earth. Jesus himself described it as the great tribulation. That time is for the future. It was for them and still is for us. But throughout these letters we discover that God has a design to deliver his own from that "coming wrath". Christians have the advantage even over the approaching crisis of the world. Much more than the assurance of heaven, or the avoidance of the agony of living, the promise is of help right now. Interwoven with the promise of John 14 that Jesus would come again is the promise that he will come to live within us now (v.17-18). The wonderful paradox Christians have is that though Christ's kingdom is yet to come when Jesus returns to this earth, he is already here with us now. Even now, He is guiding us, satisfying us, protecting us. The question this raises is, what does this mean to you? Christians have no business to be discouraged, disheartened or despondent. If we yield to any of these moods, or feelings, it is because we have neglected these great truths. But there in harassed Thessalonica, those truths were to be living, alive and sweet in the hearts of those believers. God is calling us back to this again in our day of history.

Have you turned to the living God? Are you serving and are you waiting making sure you are ready? It is far better than settling down nicely.

CHAPTER 4
Helping People 'Find' Themselves
1 Thessalonians 2: 1-12

"You know, brothers, that our visit to you was not a failure. We had previously suffered and been insulted in Philippi as you know, but with the help of our God we dared to tell you his gospel in spite of strong opposition.

For the appeal we make does not spring from error or impure motives, nor are we trying to trick you. On the contrary, we speak as men approved by God to be entrusted with the gospel. We are not trying to please men but God who tests our hearts. You know we never used flattery, nor did we put on a mask to cover up greed – God is our witness.

We were not looking for praise from men, not from you or anyone else. As apostles of Christ we could have been a burden to you, but we were gentle among you, like a mother caring for her little children. We loved you so much that we were delighted to share with you not only the gospel of God but our lives as well, because you had become so dear to us.

Surely you remember, brothers, our toil and hardship; we worked night and day in order not to be a burden to anyone while we preached the gospel of God to you. You are witnesses and so is God, of how holy, righteous and blameless we were among you who believed. For you know that we dealt with each of you as a father deals with his own children, encouraging, comforting and urging you to live lives worthy of God, who calls you into his kingdom and glory".

In 1924 at the Paris Olympic Games, Eric Liddell aroused his generation with his refusal to race on Sunday and his victory in the 400-metre race. The story was interpreted in the Academy Award-winning movie 'Chariots of Fire'. If you saw the movie, you will remember the words about the hero of the film:

"Eric Liddell, missionary, died in occupied China at the end of World War II. All of Scotland mourned."

It was one year after winning the gold medal that Eric Liddell went to China as a missionary. After teaching, he decided to engage in rural evangelism; by bicycle and by foot he carried the Gospel of Jesus Christ to the pastoral country of China. After Japan invaded China and World War II broke out, Liddell was categorised as an "enemy national" and in August 1943 he was sent to a prison camp. He was housed in a dormitory that provided a room three feet by six for each man. While a prisoner, Liddell accepted the demands of his situation and organised athletic events, taught hymns and preached God's Word. He was recalled as *"a man whose humble life combined muscular Christianity with radiant godliness." (Eric Liddell, The Disciplines of the Christian Life, Nashville Abingdon, 1985. Forward by Herbert S. Long).*

Just months before he would have been liberated, on February 21,1945, Eric Liddell died of a brain tumour. He was a national hero but more than that, he was a hero of the faith. His life continues to this day to influence others to follow Christ.

Much can be decided by the people we delight in. Everybody worships. People who idolise the rock artist, the sports star, or the person who makes a lot of money, are engaged in a form of worship. No one needs to remind us that we live in an age of fallen heroes. Instead of analysing the failures, we ought to seek out some solid role models to emulate and then decide to become the same for the generation that is looking to us. We all have a circle of influence, however young or old we are. We can make a difference in that circle.

Jesus Christ is the supreme model who constantly challenges the generations. We can also look at other good examples, like Paul. The passage in which we are spending time helps us to enter into the heart throb of this great apostle. The beauty about this passage of scripture is that it is a model for helping people *'find'* themselves.

Sometimes students will say to me, "I am taking a year out because I need to 'find' myself" It normally means they want to travel. I will often reply, "But what if in taking your year out to find yourself, you discover there is nobody really there?" There is a common presupposition that there is a self, waiting out there to be discovered. There is no such thing as a self, waiting to be *found*, only a self, waiting to be *created*. There is only one way to create a true self, to discover our real identity: turning *"to God from idols to serve the living and true God"* (1 Thessalonians 1:9).

Paul, Silas and Timothy visited the big city of Thessalonica and they were not failures. People's lives were radically revolutionised.

What was there about Paul that teaches us how to touch and change people? There are so few exciting 'role models'. We reproduce people in our brand of Christianity. The script we usually give people is reserved, timid and mediocre. What is the secret of helping people *"to live lives worthy of God"?* (1Thessalonians 2:12). We can learn from Paul.

(1) HIS COURAGE

Despite suffering insults and strong opposition in Philippi, he "dared to tell the gospel" (v.2). *Courage* is the first essential for helping anybody. In Philippi, Paul was beaten with thick sticks, stripped naked and put into stocks, a primitive form of torture. Paul's Roman citizenship rights were denied and he was ordered to leave the city. Yet, he bravely went on to Thessalonica. During the riot in Ephesus they wanted to cause him great harm, but he asked for a chance to talk to them. What courage! We sometimes find it hard to talk to one individual, let alone a rioting crowd. Religion is mentioned in conversation and we find ourselves like goldfish opening and shutting our mouth but nothing comes out. Like old Gulliver in his tales, we are tied down by tiny strands of fear, real or imagined, that prevent us from standing up and being counted for what we say we believe.

Psychologist Ruth W. Berenda and her associates carried out an interesting experiment with teenagers designed to show how a person handled group pressure. The plan was simple. They brought groups of ten adolescents into a room for an experiment. Each group of ten was commanded to raise their hands when the teacher pointed to the longest line on three separate charts. What one person in the group did not know was that the other nine in the room had been schooled ahead of time to vote for the second longest line. Regardless of the instructions they were given, once they were all together in the group, the nine were not to vote for the longest line, but rather vote for the next-to-longest line. The desire of the psychologist was to determine how one person reacted when completely surrounded by a number of people who stood against what is authentic. Time after time the self-conscious person would sit there saying a short line is longer than a long line, because he lacked the pluck to defy the group. That basic test was removed from any feeling of emotion. It was simply an analytical examination to see how a person handled group pressure. "The moral implications that attend such an experiment are startling. If your child is not taught how to stand alone when surrounded by those who put him to the test, he won't be able to cope. He or she will go through self doubt, then doubt and finally downswing into complete acquiescence." *(From Hide or Seek by James Dobson, Fleming H Revell Company, Old Tappan NJ.1979)*

The moral implications are frightening if we do not know how to stand alone. If we are not taught this when we are young, we are not going to be able to do it years later.

Paul shook the dust of Philippi off his sandals and strode over the mountains into the next big city. There was no self-pity about this man. No, "I give up, the injustice of it all. They are so spiteful, if they caught rabies they would bite me." Where did Paul get his courage? Was it his by nature?

What evangelist Billy Graham said speaking to students years ago is worth repeating: ". . . It is estimated that there are some sixty thousand serious mountain climbers in the United States. But in the upper echelon of serious climbers is a small elite group known as 'hard men'. For them climbing mountains and scaling sheer rock faces is a way of life. And their ultimate experience is called free soloing: climbing with no equipment and no safety ropes... Where are the hard men and women for Jesus? Where are those who will bring all their energies to bear for the sake of Christ?" *(Billy Graham, Faithful Witness, Urbana '84 (Downers Grove, IL: Inter Varsity Press 1985).*

When it comes to our commitment, God really wants all or nothing. The all-or-nothing principle can be illustrated with the muscles in your body. There are some muscles that can contract partially. For instance, I can contract my biceps slightly, moderately, or totally. Your heart is a muscle, but unlike other muscles, it contracts involuntarily. And every time it contracts, it contracts totally: It is an all or nothing muscle. And when it is giving all, you live. When it does not contract at all, you die. The Bible says we are to seek God with our whole heart; that means we surrender totally to Him and give Him our all. We contract all of our emotional, mental, and spiritual muscles in seeking and serving Him. It has been well said that either Jesus is Lord of all in your life, or He is not really Lord at all in your life.

Certain verses indicate Paul was not a naturally hard man. When he preached at Corinth, he said *"I came to you in weakness and fear and with much trembling."* (1 Corinthians 2:3). Corinth intimidated him. Some of you want to reach out to people and be real about your faith in your place of work, yet the pagan atmosphere inhibits you. The few times we show courage it is normally because we are backed into a corner.

Paul was like most of us by nature, a devout coward. What can turn us into *dare-lords?* I prefer that to *dare-devils.* There are three things that motivated Paul.

(i)　His purity of motive

If we are not trying to trick anyone, there is an inner confidence that comes from that. We can look the world in the eye. Whatever people think about us, we have integrity before God. Some horrible rumours were being put around about Paul and his team. The appeal they make springs from "error or impure motives... trying to trick you... flattery... put on a mask to cover up greed... looking for praise from men". (v.3-5). Paul knew, as God was his witness, he had nothing to hide.

(ii)　The power of the gospel

Four times in these verses he makes mention of the gospel *(v.2,4,8,9).* He was intensely grateful for what the Gospel was and could do for him.

Question: Why do people mess up and stay messed up? Partly because they have been educated beyond their intelligence. People believe they can plan their own lives better than God can. They end up among the living dead. Someone quipped, "I always read the obituary column every morning, to see if I am alive or dead".

There are many people *physically* existing but with no real life about them. Joking about is as much a part of life as crying. I can accept both. What I cannot accept is deadness, people who are "neither hot nor cold but lukewarm". Jesus said people being lukewarm makes him feel ill (Rev.3.16). Write down your wildest fantasy and I promise you have not even begun to imagine what eternity holds for a person who has turned from idols to the living God. (1 Corinthians 2:9). God committed this message to Paul. He considered it such an honour and privilege to declare it to others. Nothing motivates me more than to know that I have been given the greatest honour that can ever be given to a human being, to proclaim what Paul calls *"the unsearchable riches of Chri*st" (Ephesians 3:8). Could there be anything greater than that? He spoke of our blessings in these terms, "In him we have redemption through his blood, the forgiveness of sins, in accordance with the riches of God's grace" (Ephesians 1:7) A popular book several years ago was "Men are from Mars and Women are from Venus" – explaining the differences between the sexes. Perhaps I should write a book with the title, "If Men are from Mars and Women are from Venus, CHRISTIANS are from Pluto." Because Paul's word for 'riches' is *ploutos.* We really do have something different and better in Christ. That is how Paul felt, and it continually motivated him. To the Romans he said, *"I am not ashamed".* We don't say that unless we have had cause to feel ashamed. *"I am not ashamed of the gospel, because it is the* *power of God for the salvation of everyone who believes*" (Romans 1:16). That motivates.

More than that, Paul was energised by a desire to please God.

(iii)   The desire to please God

The only reason anyone has a desire to please God is because they have learned to love him. You never truly try to please God if you do not love God. You may try to please him to get something for yourself. Some have that as their motive. But if you want to really please God, if that is a strong, driving force within you, it is because you have learned that God already loves you. It is love in your relationship with God, which takes away fear.

A mother under normal circumstances would be frightened of a burning building, but with her baby in that building she may need to be restrained from foolishly rushing in. Love casts out the fear. If you need courage, don't try to summon it up from within yourself. Begin to think about the love of God, about the honour of walking with him and speaking of the truth to others. Soon you will find yourself compelled by that love. (2 Corinthians 5:14).

When William Booth began his mission work in East London in 1865, he met violent opposition that grew even more intense in 1878 when his mission became the Salvation Army. The Army historians tell us: "One Salvation Army officer came into a meeting loaded down with dead cats and rats; he explained these had been thrown at him; and that he caught and held the dead animals because if he dropped them the crowd would merely pick them up to be thrown again. Pots of human urine were often dumped on the street preachers. Beatings were not uncommon; in 1889 at least 669 Salvation Army members were assaulted – some were killed and many were maimed. Even children were not immune; hoodlums threw lime in the eyes of a child of a Salvation Army member ... They frequently stormed Salvation Army meeting halls by the hundred, broke out the windowpanes and wrecked the inside of buildings". *(William Booth, Twenty Centuries of Great Preaching, vol.5, Word Books).*

William Collier writes: "Neither age nor sex proved a barrier, for the mobs were out for blood. In Northampton, one blackguard tried to knife a passing lassie; Wolverhampton thugs flung lime in a Salvationist child's eyes. At Hastings Mrs. Susannah Beatty, one of Booth's first converts on Mile End became the Army's first martyr, buried from Clapton's Congress Hall. Reeling under a fire of rocks and putrid fish, she was kicked deliberately in the womb and left for dead in a dark alley of the Old Town. The doctor's prophecy that her injuries could prove fatal came appallingly true".

Their binding promise was this: "You must be willing that the child should spend all its life in the Salvation Army, wherever God should choose to send it, that it should be despised, hated, cursed, beaten, kicked, imprisoned, or killed for Christ sake". *(The General Next to God, William Collier, E.P. Dutton).*

Why did the Salvation Army become as the dirt of the earth? When the love of Christ controls a person, he no longer lives for himself but for Christ alone.

Someone once introduced Hudson Taylor as a great missionary who had given his life to the Orient because he loved the Chinese. Taylor slowly shook his head and answered thoughtfully, *"No not because I loved the Chinese, but because I loved God."* The love of Christ controlled him.

If our lives are characterised by ease, if we incur no problems because of our Christianity, there is every likelihood that something is wrong. John Stott has pointedly stated: "Now the church is not persecuted so much as ignored. Its revolutionary message has been reduced to a toothless creed for bourgeois suburbanites. Nobody opposes it any longer, because really there is nothing to oppose." My own conviction, for what it is worth, is that if we Christians were to compromise less, we would undoubtedly suffer more. If we were to hold fast the old-fashioned Gospel of Christ, crucified for sinners and of salvation as an absolutely free and undeserved gift, then the Cross, would again become a stumbling block to the proud. If we were to maintain the high moral standards of Jesus – of incorruptible honesty and integrity, of chastity before marriage and fidelity in it and of costly, self-sacrificial love, then there would be a public outcry that the church had returned to Puritanism. If we were to dare once more to talk plainly about the alternatives of life and death, salvation and judgement, heaven and hell, then the world would rise up in anger against such "old-fashioned rubbish". Physical violence, imprisonment and death may not be the fate of Christians in the West today, but faithfulness to Jesus Christ shall without doubt bring ridicule and ostracism. This should not surprise us, however, for we are followers of the suffering Christ. *(John Stott, Focus on Christ, London Fount Paperbacks).*

The secret of courageous activity is always in purity of motive; power of the gospel and in the desire to please God because you have realised how much he loves you.

Paul's courage alone did not change people in the city. There was something more that throbbed from him.

(2) HIS CARING

Love often has to be strong and tough. It must sometimes rebuke, but it has to learn how to do so gently. Tenderness is basic to all relationships. We never outgrow the need. Paul was *"like a mother caring for her little children"* (v.7). Mothers are a breed apart. "Mum I am going out tonight," you say. "Be sure to get in at a reasonable hour. Remember you have to get up in the morning to go to work," says Mum. "Okay mum." and off you go. You forget. You return at 4 a.m. Turning the car engine off and freewheeling into the drive, you open the front door ever so carefully. Take off your shoes you walk up the stairs avoiding the stair that creaks. Into your bedroom and you don't wake mum up. Breakfast time. Mum says, "What do you think you were doing coming in at 4 a.m. in the morning and taking your shoes off? I heard you and I noticed that you avoided the stair that creaked." You say, *"Mum I'm 55 years old!"*

Mothers keep caring. It's not easy being a mother and I would imagine being a nursing mother is particularly stressful. We have two distinct choices. One is to cultivate a small heart. If our enterprise is to avoid trials and afflictions we should hold back from enmeshing relationships and forget about august ideals. That is the most risk free way. The other option is to open ourselves to others, to become gullible to the spectrum of sorrows about which a dried up heart knows nothing.

A sentence in the diary of James Gilmour, pioneer missionary to Mongolia, must have been scribed in blood. The words were penned late in

Gilmour's life, after many years of missionary work: "In the shape of converts, I have seen no results. I have not, as far as I am aware, seen anyone who even wanted to be a Christian." *(Clyde E. Fant, Jr. and William M. Pinson, Jr. eds. Twenty Centuries of Great preaching, Word, Vol.8).*

These aching words would never have been written if James Gilmour had not decided to go for it all and give his life in caring as a servant of Christ. If he had never set out for Mongolia, he would not have found himself in this position of ostensible failure and deep disappointment.

When we have a mother's care we increase possibilities for pain. You may have already experienced this kind of hurt because of deep commitment on your part. You pursued high ideals, you gave yourself to others and your openness left you prey to sorrows that you could have ducked had you not cared like a mother. Little hearts, though they seem safe, never kick in. No one benefits from their restricted compassion and limited thinking. Mother hearts, while vulnerable, know the most joy. They leave an impression on the world.

The choice is ours. Cultivate deafness and we will never hear the clashes of life, but neither will we hear the wonderful strains of a great symphony. Propagate blindness and we will never see the ugly and hideous, but neither will we see the beauty of God's creation. Cultivate a small heart and sailing may be smooth, but we will not know the "heady winds" – the Holy Spirit working. We will not see lives change.

People, who sleep like babies, never have any. They never know what it is to be exhausted in the small hours of the morning. Jesus ministered to others when he was tired. He travelled through Samaria and came to a town called Sychar. *"Jacob's well was there and Jesus tired as he was from the journey, sat down by the well"* (John 4:6). He reacted as any exhausted man would and dropped down to relax. Jesus may have closed his eyes as he reclined by the well. He heard footsteps, looked up and saw a Samaritan woman. It would have been so easy for him to rationalise, "I have been serving hundreds and I am weary. I am a Jew and she is a Samaritan. I am a man and she is a woman. There are plenty of reasons not to talk to her. I need to relax." The choice was open to Jesus, but he didn't take it. He chose to care even though he was fatigued. A mother's heart carries on when it is at the edge of its ability. Oswald Sanders wrote, "The world is run by tired men." *(Spiritual Leadership, Moody Press).*

Nowhere in the Bible are we told to slow down and take it easy. We are to press on. We are not to be weary in well doing. Rest and entertainment must not be priorities. Most souls are won for Christ by drained people. "Playing hurt" is an expression in the sports world. While I am not countenancing playing sport when physically injured, in spiritual realities we need to learn to carry on when we don't feel like it. It has been my experience that the times I have been most used, I was at the point of fatigue. We will never do illustrious things for God until we learn to minister when we are tired.

Paul constantly worked to blaze abroad the Gospel. When he presented his testimonial to the Corinthian church, he talked about the 195 lashes he had received, about the shipwrecks, the stoning and the dangers he had borne (2 Corinthians 11). Paul gave his all in the service of Christ.

Martin Luther said he worked so hard that at night he literally fell into bed. In one account of his life, it says he did not change his bed for a year. How tired can you get!

D.L.Moody's bedtime prayer on one occasion was, "Lord I am tired. Amen".

Paul did not turn his converts over to a baby-sitter. He said, *"We loved you so much that we were delighted to share with you not only the gospel of God but our lives as well"* (v.8). A nursing mother imparts her own life to the child. The nursing mother eats the food and changes it into milk for the baby. The mature Christian feeds on the Word of God and then shares its nutriment with the youngest believers so they can grow (1 Peter 2:1-3). A nursing child can become ill through reaction to something the mother has eaten. The Christian who is feeding others must be careful not to feed on the wrong things himself.

Paul and his team were careful what they communicated as part of the body of Christ. Such was the care of Paul and his team, while preaching the gospel they *"worked night and day in order not to be a burden to anyone"* (v.9). Although Paul would accept help from established churches (cf. Philippians 4:16; 2 Corinthians 11:8), his policy when planting new churches was to pay his own way by working at his trade as a tentmaker (Acts 18:3).

Paul modelled a servant heart. Like the apostle Peter he knew that church leaders must be "eager to serve; not lording it over those entrusted to you" (1 Peter 5: 2,3)

We all know of churches that have experienced division and turmoil due to disagreement among the leaders. Sometimes pastors resign over what is called "leadership differences." That's a pleasant sounding word for a power struggle in which someone on the leadership team refuses a servant's heart. Satan loves to split churches. I've been in ministry long enough now to know that it is easy to forget I can't fix people – only God can. I heard about one pastor who finally got so fed up he quit and became an undertaker. Another pastor asked him why he moved from the pastorate to being a funeral director. He said, "I was so frustrated as a pastor. I spent years trying to straighten out Jim who was an alcoholic, but he's still drinking. I spent months trying to straighten out Mark and Jane who were having marriage problems and they still got a divorce. I spent too much time trying to straighten out John with his drug problem, but he's still addicted. Now in this job at the funeral home, when I straighten them out they stay straight!" The leaders job is not to straighten people out – only Jesus can do that. Our job is to serve them in Jesus' name. How many people know we care about their growth? Do we tolerate spiritual babies and keep feeding and caring for them? It is part of helping people truly *'find'* their real selves. Paul's *courage* and *caring* changed people because of one more thing.

(3) HIS CONSISTENCY

If we lack integrity, we do not have the power to really help. Listen to Paul: "You are witnesses and so is God, of how holy, righteous and blameless we were among you who believed" (v.10). *Holy* means in this sense, single-mindedness. He is not boasting. Whenever he speaks of his *holiness* he makes it clear that he is not responsible for it. It is the grace of God at work in him. Also he was *righteous* before others. He behaved himself. He watched his public behaviour. Finally, he was *blameless*. Do not misunderstand that. Blamelessness in Scripture never means sinless. Paul did not think of himself as sinless. What he means is, he is honest. He has dealt with all his sin. Aware of it, he does not cover it over.

Paul dealt with each member of the church *"as a father deals with his own children"* (v.11). When I was a young evangelist, I came under the leadership of Marshall Shallis. He was a man of self-discipline and strong personality. He expected 'his men', not to waste a moment of time in preaching the Gospel. When I met alone with Marshall, he was always gentle. He always spoke directly and gave me respect. I often thought of him as being like the apostle Paul. Paul could be stern and sharp, but when he was with someone alone, he was gentle. That is a mark of a true father in the faith. Marshall was someone who really cared. He prayed every day for my two daughters until his dying day. Like Paul he was encouraging, comforting and urging me to live a life *"worthy of God who called me into his kingdom of glory"* (v.12).

One of my heroes of the faith was Hudson Taylor. In 1849, he was a bored seventeen-year-old. Raised in a wealthy Christian home, he had no great interest in spiritual matters. He was very shy and spent much of his time reading. One day he was so bored he read a Christian booklet that referred to the millions of people in China who had never heard about Jesus. That day God broke his heart and from that moment, his passion was to share the love of God with the Chinese people. At age 21 he travelled to China and began trying to spread the gospel, but his first years were frustrating because few people responded to his message. One day a wise Chinese man pointed out that Hudson's English suit had extra buttons on the sleeves and backs, but there were no buttonholes – and he asked why. Hudson Taylor realized his English-style dress was distracting his listeners. From that point he was determined to learn to speak Mandarin and dress in the Chinese custom. He discovered God didn't want the Chinese to become like English Christians, but to become Chinese Christians. He later returned to England where he translated the New Testament into Chinese, and convinced others to join him in China. He returned with several other missionaries, and married one of them. Hudson Taylor faced many hardships including the death of his wife and child, but God gave him the strength to maintain his work. In one city, a middle-aged man was one of the leading officers of a reformed Buddhist group. He had long sought for the truth by studying Buddhism, Taoism, and the writings of Confucius. When Hudson Taylor shared the good news of Jesus with him, this man found the peace and truth for which he had been searching. He became a Christian and started preaching to his fellow Chinese. Shortly after his conversion, he asked Hudson Taylor how long the message of Jesus had been known in England. When he was told that it had been known for hundreds of years the man was shocked. He said, "What? For hundreds of you have had these glad tidings and only now have come to teach it to us? My father sought after the truth for more than twenty years, and died without finding it. Oh, why did you not come sooner?" Hudson Taylor was small in stature, and weak physically, but because he trusted God. Today, he is considered a spiritual giant. He devoted fifty years of his life to sharing the love of God with the Chinese. As a result of his work, when he died in 1905, there were 250 mission stations and over 100,000 new Chinese Christians.

The secret of Hudson Taylor's effectiveness was that he learned to depend upon God's strength instead of his own. If you want to experience true fulfilment in this life, you must learn this secret Hudson Taylor discovered. He wrote: "I myself, for instance, am not especially gifted, and am shy by nature, but my gracious and merciful God and Father inclined Himself to me, and when I was weak in faith He strengthened me while I was still young. He taught me in my helplessness to rest on Him, and to pray even about little things in which another might have felt able to help himself." He said that through his life, he went through three stages of understanding the secret of God's strength: "I used to ask God if He would come and help me...and then I asked God if I might come and help Him...and then I ended by asking God to do His work through me."

Have you made that discovery? If you do, the rest of your life can be the best of your life. Here's how: Become a courageous communicator of the gospel. Have the mindset of a mother when dealing with people. Calling people to holiness like a caring father. Give your life away to others – but do it in God's strength. He is the one who "calls you into his kingdom and glory" (v.12).

The challenge today is to live as Paul did. Things will begin to happen on a scale that will surprise you. You, like the man from la Mancha, "will dream the impossible dream, fight the unbeatable foe, fight with the last ounce of courage; we will go where the brave dare not go". God wants to do redoubtable things through us. Live worthy of God. Now. Today. Forever.

CHAPTER 5
The Amazing Word
1 Thessalonians 2:13-16

"And we also thank God continually because, when you received the word of God which you heard from us, you accepted it not as the work of men, but as it actually is, the word of God, which is at work in you who believe. For you, brothers, became imitators of God's churches in Judea, which are in Christ Jesus: You suffered from your own countrymen the same things those churches suffered from the Jews, who killed the Lord Jesus and the prophets and also drove us out. They displease God and are hostile to all men in their effort to keep us from speaking to the Gentiles so that they may be saved. In this way they always heap up their sins to the limit. The wrath of God has come upon them at last".

It was Sunday and a working day in that country. The room was packed with people. The preacher was connecting with the congregation. He fed the sheep as well as the giraffes! Young believers as well as the more mature were being fed by the teaching of God's Word. There were many lamps in the third-storey room, creating a stuffy atmosphere. The heat, crowd and lack of oxygen all made for sleepiness. It was all a bit too much for a young man. He nodded off into a sound sleep. Unfortunately, he was sitting on the

72

windowsill and fell headlong to the pavement three floors below. The congregation gave a shaken gasp and rushed down the outside stairs to the broken form. Eutychus was dead! Some began to cry. But not for long. 'Paul went down, threw himself on the young man and put his arms around him. "Don't be alarmed," he said." He's alive!" (Acts 20:10).

The apostle had dropped himself across the boy's lifeless form, much as did the prophets Elijah and Elisha with others. The congregation went upstairs again to continue the service. No one was sleeping now. Paul talked until daylight. "The people took the young man home alive and were greatly comforted." (Acts 20:12).

I feel sorry for young Eutychus. I am quite sure he didn't want to sleep through a sermon. How unfortunate to do it when sitting in a third-storey window and Dr. Luke is there to record the event for posterity! This is the first record of someone falling asleep in church. There have been thousands of successors, but poor Eutychus, he is the one everyone remembers.

I know what it is like to have people fall asleep on me. Some people delight in telling me that they use my recorded ministry to help soothe to sleep their little babies. "Half an hour of your voice and they are well away into dreamland," they tell me with delight. I'm glad to be of some service to fraught parents!

"I never see my preacher's eyes,
He hides their light divine,
For when he prays he shuts his own
And when he preaches, mine!"

Actually, I have a great sympathy for those who attempt to stay awake in church services. Some work such tight programmes that when they sit down in church motionless, it is the first time they have eased off all week. The elderly have developed sleep patterns which mean the service is held at the wrong time for them. Others take medication, which puts them into slumber-land. I think Eutychus was weary at the end of a hard day's work. But he wouldn't miss church for anything. He would not have died in church if he had not wanted to be there.

Falling asleep in church does not matter to me – well, not that much. It can happen for any number of reasons, both acceptable and unacceptable. What does concern me is that God's people need to be receptive to the Word of God in order to profit from it. Distinguished psychologist Paul Tournier has memorably said, "Listen to the conversation of our world, between nations as well as between couples. They are, for the most part, dialogues of the deaf." *(Paul Tournier, To Understand Each Other, Richmond, VA: John Knox Press, 1970)*

You must have experienced speaking to someone and noticing the vacant eyes. Don't you feel like knocking on their forehead and enquiring, "Hello, is anyone in?' Why are we such poor listeners? Today one of the chief reasons is that we are so busy. Our 'busyness' substitutes actions for conversation and sabotages relationships. It fills our schedules and vacates our lives of the ability to listen to anything in depth. The visual media also feed our inability to focus. This is the day of sound bytes. Watch a run-of-the-mill drama on television and you will discover that few scenes last longer than a minute. A culture so conditioned by visual changes to keep its attention has difficulty concentrating on anything, especially the plain Word. The devotional prayer of the modern man is, 'Lord speak. You have sixty seconds.'

There are many voices clamouring for our attention. Our mental circuits get over-loaded and jam. This inability to listen has huge connotations regarding the hearing of God's Word. We have got to break into all of that if we are to see adventuring growing Christians. We must take time to hear God's Word. We must prepare ourselves to receive it. In many cases Jesus required people with needs to wait days before he helped. Matthew 15:29 is an example: "Jesus left there and went along the Sea of Galilee. Then he went up on a mountainside: and sat down. Great crowds came to him bringing the lame, the blind, the crippled, the mute and many others and laid them at his feet and he healed them.' Think of the hardship he put them through. Why did he not help them at the foot of the mountain? Why make them travel such vast distances and require them to struggle up a mountainside? Because they would be more ready to receive help from him when they had put themselves out. The level of their expectation would rise with every step that they took.

Let me tell you about the *Lady Be Good,* a bomber that had seen many successful wartime missions. It was out one night on a bombing run. Returning toward home base, the crew knew how long it usually took. This night, however, there was a powerful tailwind which sent it through the air faster than normal. The crew plotted from their instruments and concluded that there must be something wrong with the dials. Their calculations told them it was time to come down and land. Their watches and clock told them this was impossible. What should they do? Should they believe their instruments and come down? They might be spotted by the enemy and shot down with anti-aircraft guns. Should they believe the clocks and come down too late, they would overshoot the airfield and die in the desert. They chose to ignore the instruments and believed the gut-level feeling. They stayed up. They overshot the airfield and their plane was found days later, crashed in the desert. All the crewmen had died.

The story of *the Lady Be Good* is a picture of life. We are all on the *Lady Be Good.* In making the determination on where and when to land we have to make choices. We must choose whether to look outside ourselves – whether we trust our feelings or whether we look for an instrument panel. The Bible offers itself as a reliable guide to truth. The Bible is the 'instrument panel'. It tells us where we came from, where we are and where we are going. We must decide whether we accept the 'reading' we get from it.

Charles Haddon Spurgeon said, 'A Bible which is falling apart usually belongs to someone who is not." When all is said and done, it is God's Word that is basic to all the good changes in our lives. Paul knows this to be true and testifies to that fact. Whatever else we do, spending time in our Bible is never wasted. This is a resource for pressured times.

Think of the ways in which the Word of God blesses from Psalm 119. If you are a student of the Bible, you no doubt know that this is the longest chapter of the Bible. It is also an acrostic or alphabet psalm. That fact is not immediately apparent in the English translations, but it is very clear if you look at the Hebrew text. When the psalmist (who is not named in the text) sat down to write, he used the 22 letters of the Hebrew alphabet as his guide. He ended up writing 22 eight-verse stanzas, one for each letter of the alphabet. But the acrostic structure, though unique, is not the most notable fact about this psalm. Its most unusual feature is its theme: The glories of the Word of God. The longest psalm in the Bible is a psalm in praise of the Bible! Every verse (with only one or two exceptions) contains a direct reference to the Bible. To give variety, the psalmist uses at least nine different terms to describe God's Word: law, testimonies, judgements, precepts, statutes, commandments, ordinances, promises and word. Those words are synonyms for God's spoken and written revelation. They call us to praise God for the gift of his Word. Taken from a New Testament perspective, we should praise God for his written Word that reveals the incarnate Word, the Lord Jesus Christ, who is our Saviour and the source of eternal life.

Consider just two statements in Psalm 119.

First, "How sweet are your promises to my taste, sweeter than honey to my mouth" (v.103).

In those days honey was the universal sweetener. Back then people used honey the way we use sugar and artificial sweeteners. The writer is telling us that he has a "sweet tooth" for God's Word. To most of us, that is an unusual and perhaps even a strange thought. To us sweetness speaks of chocolate cake and ice-cream. What does he mean? As we ponder the words of the Bible one by one, phrase by phrase, verse by verse, they become sweet to us.

Think of hard confectionery. How do you eat it? You put it in your mouth and let it dissolve slowly. As it dissolves, the sweetness fills your mouth. If you try to put ten pieces in your mouth, they won't fit and you'll end up spitting them out. The sweetness you seek comes slowly, one piece at a time. Martin Luther said the way to study the Bible is to pick a verse and then shake it like you shake a fruit tree. If you keep shaking a verse, sooner or later the fruit will fall in your lap. Luther also said if the fruit doesn't fall, go to another verse. Eventually you will find a verse where the fruit falls in abundance. There you can stop and feast on God's Word. How desperately we need this. We live in a garish, loud, mean, harsh, strident, ugly and abusive age. We need to turn aside from the sounds of the world and fill our minds with something beautiful. Once the Word of God becomes sweet to you, you will become a sweeter person. And that sweetness comes to us as we spend time with our Lord in his Word.

Secondly, the Psalmist says something which sounds odd to us. "I gain understanding from your precepts; therefore I hate every wrong path" (v.104). I am sure if we were writing this stanza, we would end it with the part about sweetness. That's a nice place to finish. Much nicer than "Holy Hatred." But the Christian life is more than sweetness. There is also a hard edge to our faith. Whether we like it or not, we live in an ugly world where evil people do terrible things. And even apparently nice people can sometimes be incredibly cruel. If we are going to grow spiritually, we must learn to hate evil. Take a moment to contrast the end of the stanza with the beginning. Verse 97 says, "Oh, how I love your law!" and verse 104 concludes with "therefore I hate every wrong path." One essential part of Christian discipleship is learning to hate evil. Before we can fully love God's Word, we must also hate what God hates. If we love God's law, we will hate every false path. We will never learn what is true unless we also learn what is false and turn from it. There is a very practical ramification from this truth. If you ignore the Bible, sin will not seem very bad to you. Apart from the Bible, sin will seem "sort of bad" and "not very good."

There is no contradiction between verses 103 and 104. They belong together. Loving the Word makes us sweeter and stronger at the same time. As God's Word grows sweeter, every false way will become more repulsive to us.

Paul helps us to explore the right attitude to the Word of God.

APPRECIATE THE WORD

Paul continually thanked God that when the Thessalonians heard Paul, Silas and Timothy, "you accepted it not as the word of men, but as it actually is, the word of God" (v.13).

If the Bible is God's Word (and it is), then we must bow in submission. We should never say, "I know what the Bible says, but . . ."

This reminds me of the story of the church that was going through a difficult controversy. Agreement between people was hard to find. At a Church Member meeting there were arguments about the minutes of the previous meeting. When the pastor read a scripture passage, an older man stood to his feet and said, "Mr. Chairman, I move that the Bible stand approved as read." Good point. It is not up for a vote.

In the gospels, there were only three occasions when God spoke directly to people. The experience amazed everybody who heard, incapacitating them with fear. God spoke aloud when Jesus was baptised. Then, when our Lord was on the Mount of Transfiguration with Peter, James and John, God spoke to them directly. Again during that last week in Jerusalem, when Jesus declared that he was about to die, the Father spoke from the heavens. But he does not do that very frequently. Most of the time he speaks through human beings and he does it in different ways. Jeremiah says that the Word of God came to him like a "burning in his bones." It was something he had to utter; he could not keep quite about it. Elijah announced that the Word of God came to him like a "still small voice". It probably was not a voice at all but a quiet realisation that God was talking to him. Daniel said that God spoke to him in "vision and dreams in the night", and he went on to interpret those strange and marvellous dreams and visions. Moses said that when God communicated with him, he spoke to him "face to face, like man speaks with friends". That does not mean that Moses saw God, because the Bible also says that no one has ever seen God. What Moses was saying was that the communication was so clear it was as though God was speaking directly to him. The apostle Peter wrote, "Holy men of old spoke as they were carried by the Spirit". This is the most common way in which the word of God has come to us. Unarguably, that is the way the Thessalonian Christians experienced it. Paul stood up and began to speak to them and as he spoke they were aware that what they were hearing was far more than the words of a mere man. They were hearing God's Word.

This raises a problem, of course, there are plenty of phoneys around, false prophets claiming to speak a message from God. The Mormon prophet Joseph Smith claimed that an angel named Moroni appeared to him and revealed things to him. Smith claimed to have been given special spectacles to enable him to read a language written on golden tablets which he would find buried in a hillside. Many people believe that claim, even though the book he wrote is vastly different in its teaching from the Bible. How can we tell when God has really spoken and when we are hearing form impostors? The scriptures help us.

First we must remember that God's accomplishments in the world always agree with his Words. God never acts oppositely to his Word. If someone promises you something that the Word of God does not promise, you can know directly that you have heard a fraud speaking.

Furthermore, when a prophet predicts that a certain event will occur in the future and it does not happen, that person is a phoney. The Bible makes the astounding demand that when it makes a prediction it must be one hundred percent correct or you can disregard it; it is not the Word of God. Gauged by that standard, some of the forecasts we hear today are rather laughable. The clear mark of the Word of God is its exactness. It accords with fact.

Check your *appreciation* level for the Word of God.

A teacher quizzed a group of university bound pupils and learned some astounding things about the Bible:

Sodom and Gomorrah were lovers,
Jezebel was Ahab's donkey,
The New Testament Gospels were written by Matthew, Mark, Luther and John,
Eve was created from an apple,
Jesus was baptised by Moses and
Golgotha was the name of the giant who slew the apostle David. *(Adapted from Max Anders, The Good Life, Word Books 1993)*

That would be funny, comic, were it not so desperately sad. Learning the Word of God is not quick and easy. But it is the only way to go for spiritual growth. Much of the stress Christians experience originates between their ears. They need to get their minds sorted out. Put your hand on your head. Tap it gently. Say, "That's where my problem is. Right between my ears." God wants your whole way of thinking transformed until it is Christ-like. It is a process of maturing and this takes time. The Bible is not a big book. It can be read in one hundred hours.

Appreciating the word of God is not enough. We must *apply* it.

APPLY THE WORD

The Thessalonian Christians heard and believed the Word of God (v.13). It became part of their lives. To merely memorise or mentally accept it does not change anyone. We learn to trust God by trusting God. We must do something with what we hear.

"In 1787 Captain Bligh took the ship The Bounty, on a voyage around the world to collect bread-fruit trees. When he reached Tahiti in the central Pacific he found a veritable paradise. Soon every sailor had a girlfriend. There was quite a deal of grumbling when Bligh announced that after a few months in this heaven on earth, they were leaving. Not many days out of Tahiti, Bligh woke up to find himself looking down the barrel of a gun. Bligh and eighteen officers were put in a small boat without maps. Fletcher Christian and eight mutineers took the ship back to Tahiti and the pretty ladies. There they persuaded not eight but twelve girls to go with them. They set off again for fear of being caught. They had no plans and came across Pitcairn Island. It was another island paradise. They took as many of their things as possible onto the island and then set fire to the ship. What looked like paradise turned out to be ten years of hell. One of the sailors used a copper kettle to make a distillery. They drank the 'fire-water' made from the tree roots. The men spent days, weeks and months on end 'plastered' on spirits. Some of the men went mad and became like animals. They fought among themselves. One jumped off a cliff. After several years there were only two men left. Edward Young and Alexander Smith. Young was old, ill and asthmatic. One night, Young went to the ship's chest and at the bottom among the papers, he found a book. It was a leather-bound old, mildewed and worm-eaten Bible. He had not read for years and Smith could not read at all. So Young taught him. The two men, frightened, disillusioned and utter wrecks, together read the Bible. They started at Genesis. They saw from the Old Testament that God was holy and they were sinful. They did their best to pray. The little children were the first to come to the men. They noticed a change in them. Then the children brought the women. They sat and listened to them read. During this time Young died. Smith then came to the New Testament. Something important happened to him as he read the story

85

of Jesus in the Bible. "I had been working like a mole for years," he said "and suddenly it was as if the doors flew open and I saw the light and I met God in Jesus Christ and the burden of my sin rolled away and I found new life in Christ."

Eighteen years after the mutiny on The Bounty, a ship from Boston came across the island of Pitcairn and the captain went ashore. He found a community of people who were godly. They had a love and peace about them that he had never seen before. When the captain got back to the United States he reported that in all his travels he had never seen or met a people who were so good, gracious or so loving. They had been changed by the message of the Bible." *(Graham Twelfree, Drive The Point Home, Monarch Publications 1994).*

Paul states that the Thessalonians accepted what they heard "not as the word of men, but as it actually is, the word of God, which is at work in you who believe" (v.13). The power of the Word of God is connected to a believing heart. The word is energised within us, as we believe it. It is like a field that yields a good crop. We hear the message outwardly, we welcome it inwardly by faith. It will produce a harvest in our life.

Check List: I *appreciate* the Word of God.
I *apply* the Word of God.

Scripture has no magical properties. It is ineffective unless received. Paul knew that the message had brought life because these new believers were willing to suffer for the truth. If you believe it is true you will prove it by being willing to suffer. A tragedy of Christian suffering is that it comes from the least likely source. Some of their own countrymen, the Jews, were making it tough (v.14). Sometimes parents are happy for their son or daughter to attend a Church, as long as they don't get too involved. Religion is the biggest enemy of Christianity. Those who claim to be near God often become the greatest enemy to those who come near to God. Jesus came to bring men to God and they killed the Lord Jesus (v.15). There is no religious bigotry in that accusation. Nowhere does the Bible impeach all the Jews for what a few Jews did in Jerusalem and Judea when Christ was crucified and the church was established. The Romans also shared in the trial and death of Christ and please note, it was *our* sins that sent him to the cross (Isaiah 53:6). There is no place in the Christian faith for anti-Semitism. Paul himself loved his fellow Jews and sought to help them (Acts 24:17; Romans 9:1-5).

What happened to the Lord Jesus and the prophets occurred to Paul, Silas and Timothy (v.15).

ANGRY AT THE WORD

Why the reaction against this remarkable word of God?

First, it is clear from Scriptures that the gospel ignores all human achievement. God is totally unimpressed by degrees, wealth, or any other trappings of power. Everybody must come to him the same simple way: by admitting they cannot help themselves and by accepting salvation as a gift from the hand of God through Jesus Christ. Other religions find this claim to be offensive. Why, I do not know, because much of life is like that. The laws of electricity must be carefully observed before you dare fiddle with electric currents and they do not show regard for persons. You cannot make up your own rules. The telephone company insists you get the correct number in order when you use the telephone. You do not have the freedom of arranging them to your own liking. You must get them just right. God insists that there is only one way to be attuned with him and that is through Jesus Christ. That makes a lot of people very irate.

Second, the gospel arouses fierce opposition in that it exposes human arrogance. There is an autonomous spirit in each of us that says, "I don't need any help. I can make it on my own." We are all blameworthy of this in varying degrees, but we keep it under control for fear of recrimination or out of the desire not to be known as inflexible. But if the constraints are removed, that pride will suddenly break out in the most terrible form of maliciousness and vindictiveness.

Third, the reason why the gospel stirs opposition is that it forgives brazen sinners; those who deserve death and hell in the eyes of the world. The Pharisees were outraged because Jesus received adulterers, prostitutes and outcasts, while they themselves, decent ethical people, were barred. That is why they finally killed Jesus. Many oppose the gospel because it appeals to the unrespectable. But that is its glory: it can change anyone who will receive it in humility and contriteness.

The tragedy is, if we refuse a deeper experience of God, we become jealous of those who receive it. I may attend Church for a year and another person experiences God in a richer way than I! And I close my heart. This happened to Jews in Paul's day. They tried hard to keep Paul and his team from "speaking to the Gentiles so that they may be saved. In this way they always heap up their sins to the limit. The wrath of God has come upon them at last" (v.16). Not only did it come in the spiritual darkness they experienced, another judgement was about to fall when in A.D.70 the Roman armies besieged Jerusalem, destroyed the city and the temple and ended the period of God's patience with his people during the ministry of the apostles (Matthew 22:1-11).

Paul knew that was coming. God had in great forbearance, allowed them to – "heap up their sins to the limit" (v.16). He waited till the final moment. God is not an angry, acrimonious being who flings thunderbolts of judgement upon men at any slight annoyance. No, he gives us a chance to wake up and see what is happening to us and waits for us to change. But if we do not, there comes a time when he forces us to live with the aftermath of our actions. Catastrophes hit in order to agitate us and rouse us. That is what Paul is writing about. God's wrath brings upon us terrible consequences as a last-ditch manoeuvre to open our eyes to reality. The thrust of what God is saying is this. If we do not welcome the Word of God, others with less religious instruction and background will pass us by. If God says something to you, go with him. If you do not, you will soon be an enemy to those who do.

I cannot finish this chapter without making reference to the startling statement to those who don't go with God's Word. "You diligently study the Scriptures because you think that by them you possess eternal life. These are the Scriptures that testify about me, yet you refuse to come to me to have life" (John 5:39-40). He chose a technical word that had been used to describe the too extreme studiousness of the scribes and others who laboured over the Scriptures. Though they always had their noses in the Bible, they never got beyond the parchment and ink. The biblical scholars of the day rejected Jesus when he came to them.

Imagine that you are standing on the observation floor of a building overlooking the city, just as the sun is setting. You are enjoying the beauty of the sun on the river when someone next to you says, "Isn't this a marvellous window? Do you see how it is set in steel and how the glass is tinted?" As he unfolds his pocket-knife and begins to scrape a corner of the window, he offers: "I am going to do a chemical analysis of the window. If you will give me your address, I will let you know what the window is made of." Naturally, you think the man is a bit strange, because he has missed the purpose of the window – to view the sunset and the city.

While I am committed to detailed study of the Word of God, I do not believe this study is only for the sake of literary analysis, or culling details. The Bible is the 'window' through which we look to see the realities of Christ.

The text itself is not the Truth. Black spots on white paper are not Beethoven's sonata. It's not until the ink marks are put into practice and performed, when life and sound are added, that the score takes on life and transports those who hear it. The Bible is the score of the Creator who continues to speak to the church and point us to the Conductor in life-giving ways. It's quite possible to know the Scriptures and not know the God. It is like knowing about someone and not knowing Him. The Bible is best read as a love letter from God, not a question book or an answer book, not a systematic theology or a scientific textbook. The main subject of the Bible is God's relationship with what God most loves — God's creation and creatures.

John Broadus was one of the great men in American church history. He resigned from the presidency of the University of Virginia to found the Southern Baptist Seminary in Louisville, Kentucky. His work was interrupted by the Civil War and when he returned to Louisville, he had only seven students, yet he was a committed teacher and wrote one of the greatest books on the art of preaching for a blind student in his class. Three weeks before he died, Broadus was before his class. The Scripture reading for that day was Acts 18:24: "Apollos, a native of Alexandria, came to Ephesus. He was a learned man, with a thorough knowledge of the Scriptures". Broadus went on to say, "Gentlemen, we must be like Apollos, mighty in the Scriptures." A student later said that a hush fell on that class as Broadus stood and repeated, "Mighty in the Scriptures, mighty in the Scriptures, mighty in the Scriptures!" *(A.T. Robertson, Types of Preachers in the New Testament, George H. Doran).*

How do we gain a thorough knowledge of the Scriptures? How do we continue to hear the voice of God through them? An episode in the life of Jesus gives us an answer. As antagonism to him increased, He spoke more often in parables. On one particular day, he gave the mystery parables. After the first one, his disciples asked him, "Why do you speak to the people in parables?" He replied, "The knowledge of the secrets of the kingdom of heaven has been given to you, but not to them. Whoever has will be given more and he will have an abundance. Whoever does not have, even what he has will be taken from him" (Matthew 13:10-12).

In essence Christ was saying, "If you do not put truth in motion, it will be taken away. If you act on the truth, you will receive more." We need to write this axiom in our hearts. When we frequently hear the truth but do not answer to it, we can be sure it will be taken away. This is why I fear for the person who does not know Christ, but can complacently join a congregation, hear the truths and never respond; the time will come when he will be unable to embrace the truth. As a believer I have the responsibility to respond to the truths of the Word of God. When I am moved by something I hear, I make a memorandum to myself so that I will be sure to put into action the truth I have received.

Eutychus fell asleep in church, but he was not asleep to God's Word. He did what he could to place himself in a position to hear and respond. What about us?

CHAPTER 6
Stressed Out But Strengthened
1 Thessalonians 2:17-3:13

"But brothers, when we were torn away from you for a short time (in person, not in thought), out of our intense longing we made every effort to see you. For we wanted to come to you – certainly. I, Paul did again and again – but Satan stopped us. For what is our hope, our joy, or the crown in which we will glory in the presence of our Lord Jesus when he comes? Is it not you? Indeed, you are our glory and joy.

So when we could stand it no longer, we thought it best to be left by ourselves in Athens. We sent Timothy, who is our brother and God's fellow worker in spreading the gospel of Christ, to strengthen and encourage you in your faith, so that no one would be unsettled by these trials. You know quite well that we were destined for them. In fact, when we were with you, we kept telling you that we would be persecuted. And it turned out that way, as you well know. For this reason, when I could stand it no longer, I sent to find out about your faith. I was afraid that in some way the tempter might have tempted you and our efforts might have been useless. But Timothy has just now come to us from you and has brought good news about your faith and love. He has told us that you always have pleasant memories of us and that you long to see us, just as we also long to see you.

Therefore, brothers, in all our distress and persecution we were encouraged about you because of your faith. For now we really live, since you are standing firm in the Lord. How can we thank God enough for you in return for all the joy we have in the presence of our God because of you? Night and day we pray most earnestly that we may see you again and supply what is lacking in your faith.

Now may our God and Father himself and our Lord Jesus clear the way for us to come to you.

May the Lord make your love increase and overflow for each other and for everyone else, just as ours does for you. May he strengthen your hearts so that you will be blameless and holy in the presence of our God and Father when our Lord Jesus comes with all his holy ones."

Emotions can do some strange things. Dr. James Dobson tells of a group of tough U.S. marines dropped behind the lines during the Vietnam War. They were told, "This is a Vietcong area, hold the hill and dig in." At 1.30 that night the attack began. They fought all night long, the night sky lit up with the firepower. Early the next morning when the Vietcong had withdrawn they checked for bodies. Nobody was there. They had imagined the whole thing. Someone got nervous and fired, causing a return of fire from the other side of the camp. They fought the night – and won. Your mind will tend to conform to your emotional feelings even if the emotions are invalid.

In this section of Paul's letter he gives the inside story on his tangled emotions. I am so glad that Paul was honest. There were times when he was afraid. There were occasions when he was bubbling with joy.

I wonder where the idea arose that Paul was stern and cold? You cannot read this letter without sensing the warmth of his heart and the depth of his love. At the time he wrote this letter, he was ministering alone in the city of Corinth. He was feeling the loneliness of that moment. Being far away from loved ones is a very unpleasant experience. Forgetting the danger that had driven him from Thessalonica and the cruelty he had experienced there, he longed to be with them again.

Already in this chapter we have three sources of opposition to the apostle: Opposition from the state (v.2); opposition from society (v.14); and here, opposition from Satan. While this might look like three enemies, it is really only one. Other Scriptures indicate that the state and society are often the channels of the devil's attempt to hinder the spread of the good Word of God. This is what Paul encountered.

We sometimes get the idea that the ideal Christian life is to be beautifully even. I don't find that in the life of Jesus (John 11:35). A little girl said to her mother, "Mummy, do all fairy stories begin 'once upon a time?" "No, dear," she replied, "some begin, 'When I became a

Christian I came to the end of all my troubles." How true. Becoming a Christian you did come to the end of all your troubles – this end. There are more to follow. You have simply exchanged one set of troubles for another. The difference is, you are getting all of your troubles over now with none to come in eternity, which is just when the unbelievers will begin.

Paul is open about his stressed-out emotions. More important than his struggles are the actions he took when he experienced emotional stress.

Consider Paul's emotional temperature. Notice how it goes up and down.

HE BATTLES WITH ANXIETY

He had been in such a tense and dangerous situation he left Thessalonica quickly and quietly. Some believer's were probably saying, Paul is a fly-by-night. He can't stand the heat. He has left us in our hour of need. Paul says: "We were torn away from you" (v.17) Paul dealt with the Thessalonians with the gentleness of a mother (2:7) and with the firmness of a father (2:11). The phrase 'torn away' is a very powerful image that literally means, "When we were made orphans." Paul was a mother and father and now feels like a child who has been ripped away from his parents. Because of intense Jewish opposition, he was run out of town. His body left them but not his thoughts. His heart was still in Thessalonica. He wanted his body to return to where his heart was. Even though our hearts are with people, that is not enough. We need physical contact. Paul felt he had not said a proper goodbye and longed to return. Some of the new believers were beginning to question his motives. "If he loved us why did he leave us? And why doesn't he come back to see us again?"

Paul truly had a deep love for people. He so loved the Philippian Church he said, "I desire to depart and be with Christ, which is better by far; but it is more necessary for you that I remain in the body" (Philippians 1:23-24). Love for the Corinthian Church led him to write, "I will very gladly spend for you everything I have and expend myself as well" (2 Corinthians 12:15).

You know how good parents talk when away from their young children, often wondering and worrying about their welfare. "We made every effort to see you, for we wanted to come to you – certainly I, Paul did, again and again – but Satan stopped us," says Paul (1 Thessalonians 2:18).

The phrase, "Satan stopped us," is a military metaphor for an army that sets up a roadblock in order to impede the enemy. It can also refer to the breaking up of a road so that it becomes impassable. Every time Paul tried to return to Thessalonica he ran headlong into a satanic obstruction. I would love to know the answer to certain questions. How did he know it was

Satan? How could he be so sure? Shall I tell you why Satan does this? If Satan can keep Christians apart, he will. If he can keep someone who can meet your spiritual needs away from you, he will. I don't know whether it was sickness. Perhaps it was difficulties crossing the frontiers. If Satan can stop Christians building each other up he will.

Paul has a double desire. He wanted to be present with them on earth and proud of them in heaven. That is one Christian meeting Satan cannot stop – when our Lord Jesus Christ comes. Paul wants to be proud of them then. "What is our hope, our joy, or the crown in which we will glory in the presence of our Lord Jesus Christ when he comes? Is it not you?" (v.19).

When you face Jesus what will be your glory and joy? There are many things we purr over now that will count for nothing then. You may have passed your exams, been successful in business, bought a delightful and spacious house. In that day your glory will be the number of people brought closer to God through your witness. It was Howard Hendricks who said, "Only two things in this world are eternal – the Word of God and people. It only makes sense to build your life around those things that will last forever." Because this is true, we are wise to make sure the Bible is in us and that we are investing our lives in people. Our goal should be to go to heaven and take as many people as possible with us. How you will burst with legitimate pride in the presence of Jesus. With legitimate pride Paul says, "You are our glory and joy". That is Paul's ambition: what is yours? If you have the same desire as Paul you will understand what he says next.

IN HIS ANXIETY PAUL ALSO EXPRESSED FEELING OF DISTRESS.

Paul's team had gone further south to Athens. Some people say, "No news is good news". I don't think so. You tend to imagine the worse. Paul was not only interested in starting a church. He was prepared to send Timothy back to them to help their spiritual growth. Paul felt like death warmed up. He was distressed by two things:

First, that they would become discouraged.

Thank God for honest preachers who clearly state that Christianity exchanges one set of troubles for another. When Paul was with them, he kept telling that they would be persecuted (see v.4). It is one thing to know it in your head but still another when it happens to you. For every Christian, life is a battle. I have noticed that our Lord often gives a special protection to a new believer – what we might call a honeymoon period. Then he lets us live in the real world with its indifference and rejection of the Gospel. Paul is worried the believers at Thessalonica will be "unsettled by these trials" (v.3).

Second, they would be tempted.

Satan is winning against Paul. He has been prevented from returning. When the going gets tough we can be tempted to check out. Paul was a good evangelist. He was afraid his "efforts might have been useless" (v.5). Tough times can tempt us to give up.

Paul was so worried that these new Christians would crumble that he sent Timothy to find out if they were still standing strong. Trials can cause casualties even for the most courageous of Christians. Under pressure we can develop wrong attitudes, and slide down the slippery slope of despair.

To the emotions of *anxiety* and *distress*, Paul also had more positive emotions.

A ZEST FOR LIVING

"Timothy has just come to us from you and has brought good news about your faith and love." says Paul (v.6). This is the only time the word: 'gospel' is used in the New Testament other than for the message of the Gospel of Jesus Christ. "He (Timothy) told us you always have pleasant memories of us and that you long to see us, just as we also long to see you". (v.6) Christian workers often hear about the problems and that can lower morale. But to hear someone going on in faith and love helps God's servant to know it is worthwhile after all.

Nothing is more encouraging for a Christian worker than to learn that his converts are "standing firm"(v.8). Think now of the person most instrumental in your spiritual growth. Can you contact them?

The faithfulness of Paul's converts was a life and death matter for Paul. "For now we really live," he says (v.8). This letter must have been written as soon as Timothy had returned. If you can contact the person who has spiritually helped you, who knows – you might just put new life into them.

That sent Paul's emotions soaring.

THE WONDERFUL EMOTION HE FEELS NOW IS – JOY.

"How can we thank God enough for you in return for all the joy we have in the presence of our God because of you" (v.9). Paul was not working up a state of pseudo-fervour. Where you do not experience profound emotion when praying, just ignore the emotion and keep praying. Paul prayed earnestly. Nothing flippant, "Bless me and my wife: son John and his wife: us four and no more". He takes time to think deeply on their needs.

Paul prays frequently.

"Night and day we pray" (v.10). He puts it this way in 5:17, "Pray continually." Corrie Ten

Boom, who was held in a concentration camp, writes this about prayer, "When a Christian shuns fellowship with other Christians, the devil smiles. When he stops reading the Bible, the devil laughs. When he stops praying, the devil shouts for joy." *(Prayer Powerpoints, Victor Books, p.109).*

While Paul is making and mending tents, his lips are not moving but his heart is communing.

Paul prays fervently.

"Night and day we pray most earnestly" (v.10). He is going above and beyond all normal measures. It can be translated, 'super abundantly'. There is no power in prayer – the power is in God not our prayers. But our prayers lay the track along which God's power can come. If we do not lay the track the effects will not be known through us. If we are casual about our praying little will be achieved. Half-hearted prayers produce half-hearted results. God says, "You will seek me and find me when you seek me with all your heart" (Jeremiah 29:13).

Paul prays specifically.

He wants to see them again (see v.10). A Physical blockage to being with them did not prevent him from praying. Tell God exactly what it is you would like done. Some of our prayers are not answered because we are not precise enough in our requests (James 4:2).

C.S. Lewis imagines a hellish conversation in his famous Screwtape Letters, "It is, no doubt, impossible to prevent his praying for his mother. But we have the means of rendering the prayers innocuous. Make sure that they are very 'spiritual', that he is always concerned with the state of her soul and never with her rheumatism." *(Screwtape Letter, C.S. Lewis, Fontana).*

Check how specific your prayers are. Would you know when God has answered? Do you pray too generally? What helped him to keep praying? Spot my deliberate mistake: "night and day I pray most earnestly that I may see you again". It is not *'I'* (singular) but *'we'* (plural). *"We* pray most earnestly that *we* may see you again" (v.10). This is not a private prayer.
He prayed corporately.

Consider what Jesus said: "This is how you should pray: 'Our Father in heaven'." Not "My Father. It is a pagan idea to think that we can ever pray privately. We are joined with the angels of heaven every time we pray (Revelation 4:8).

What more can a group prayer meeting do? Surely, if we all pray like fury for the same thing even if we are not physically with one another, that should be enough. No! A prayer meeting is a school, fireplace and powerhouse. We learn how to pray in the company of other believers. (Luke 11:1). We help one another to keep spiritual fervour (Romans 12:11). Corporate prayer releases greater power (Acts 4:31). Can you imagine the prayer meetings Paul, Silas and Timothy had?

Paul wants to see the Thessalonian believers again. "and supply what is lacking in your faith" (v.10). The word he uses is used for the mending of nets (Mark 1:19). Our faith never reaches perfection; there is always need for adjustment and growth. We go "from faith to faith" (Romans 1:17). Faith is like a muscle: it gets stronger with use.

Paul prayed to overcome satanic hindrance.

Probably five years passed before the prayer was answered. But it was answered. Have you felt like giving up on prayer? Don't. Pray some more.

Paul's request was also that their love might "increase and overflow for each other and for everyone else" (v.12). Times of trial can be times of selfishness. Persecuted people often become very self-centred and demanding. What life does to us depends on what life finds in us; and nothing reveals the true inner man like the fire of affliction. Some people build walls in times of trial and shut themselves off. Others build bridges and draw closer to the Lord and his people. This was Paul's prayer for these believers and God answered it. (2Thessalonians 1:3).

The entire Trinity is involved in this prayer. Paul addressed the Father and Son in verse 11. In verse 12 "the Lord" may refer to the Holy Spirit, since "our Lord" at the end of verse 13 certainly refers to Jesus Christ. If this is so, then this is the only prayer in the New Testament directed to the Holy Spirit. The Bible pattern of prayer is: to the Father, through the Son and in the Spirit.

Paul wants his converts to stand "blameless and holy in the presence of God and Father when our Lord Jesus comes with all his holy ones" (v.13). Since all believers will be transformed to be like Christ when he returns (1 John 3:2), Paul could not be referring to our personal condition in heaven. He was referring to our lives here on earth as they will be reviewed at the Judgement Seat of Christ. We will never face our sins in heaven, for they are remembered against us no more (Romans 8:1; Hebrews 10:14-18). But our works will be tested and you cannot separate conduct from character.

It is time for a review.

This passage takes just a few moments to read. But what an emotional helter-skelter we ride. *Anxiety, distress, zest for living, joy, dissatisfaction.* Whatever emotions we experience now, that is nothing to what we will feel when Jesus returns.

The lessons.

There are many lessons we can learn from Paul's emotional graph in this section of his letter. Let's look at a few.

Emotional downsides are normal.

They are not wrong nor are they avoidable. Paul could not stop the trials and persecution. There are certain circumstances that are beyond our control. Anxious feelings are therefore inevitable. For every up there comes a down. That is how we are made. It helps to roll with the blow when you acknowledge this. As you listen to a person sharing his emotions be careful to refrain from telling him how he should feel. There are no 'shoulds' or 'should nots' with feelings; they just are. You may not understand another's emotions, but don't deny or ignore them.

Don't wallow in an emotional downer.

Every anxiety and distress demands we ask what action we must take to resolve the stress. The resolution to Paul's stressed-out feeling was to send Timothy to find out what has actually happening. Some people avoid finding out what is happening for fear that what they fear is a reality, so they just go on worrying. Often the fear is unjustified. And even if it is based on reality, finding out what has caused the problem most often enables us to solve it and thereby overcome our fear and anxiety.

If you have pleasant memories, don't have a short memory.

Look for opportunities to show appreciation in tangible ways. Encourage one another. This is required of all Christians (1 Thessalonians 5:11).

In his play *Pygmalion,* George Bernard Shaw insists that a lady and a flower girl differ not by the way they act, but by how they are treated. In My Fair Lady, the musical of Shaw's play, the delightful flower girl Eliza Doolittle expresses these sentiments after she has undergone the transformation from pauper to a much-praised lady. She contrasts the encouraging style of the sympathetic Colonel Pickering with the unyielding bantering of her tutor, Professor Henry Higgins. Then she concludes that she never ceases to be a lady around the colonel because he never fails to treat her as such, that Professor Higgins' rough treatment of her prevents her from ever fulfilling the part around him. The encouragement process provides energy to blaze a path of improvement.

When you feel low because of a 'no-go' sign, don't give up.

Some Christians are tempted to interpret all barriers to achieving difficult goals as God's barriers. "If God wanted me to accomplish this goal he would have opened the door and made it happen." If that were true, why did Paul say: "Satan stopped us" (1 Thessalonians 2:18)?

Some things are wrong. We are stupid to persevere. Some plans are right. We should set up alternative plans and persevere. God will clarify the difference when we are open to him.

Satanic opposition is permitted by God.

The book of Job says that Satan had to come before God and get permission from him to afflict Job's body (Job 2:6). This man lost everything – his family, home and wealth. He suffered terribly from boils, which covered his whole body. But God had allowed it. The end of the book reveals what was accomplished by that suffering, but it was all hidden for the moment from Job's eyes. So too, it is hidden for our eyes, but the Bible reveals there is a malevolent power of evil at work. There are demonic beings, master manipulators that are able to lead people about, putting thoughts into their minds and planting obstacles in the path of the gospel. God permits this for this reason: these things are used by him.

Opposition is his method of training.

Affliction, suffering, pain and heartache are often God's way of getting our attention. Many of you have gone through that. You paid little attention to him until you suffered a time of great heartache. Then you began to hear what he was saying to you. God uses opposition to train us, not only that, to give us an opportunity to overcome trouble, to rise above it.

Don't give up!

Keep praying with and for one another.

Don't settle for the status quo. Paul's prayer was answered in the affirmative, because during his third missionary journey, on his way back from Jerusalem, he did visit Macedonia again. Thomas Chalmers was right when he said that, "Prayer does not just enable us to do a greater work for God. Prayer is a greater work for God." Paul prayed without ceasing for his loved ones in Thessalonica. Night and day!

My priorities.

I don't know about you, but the example of Paul and the mix of his emotions prompt me to evaluate my priorities. We sometimes get bogged down in the daily routine of living and forget the essential task of our life. If we begin now to allow the Spirit of God to use us to win men, women, boys and girls to faith, love and hope in the Saviour, what high emotions there will be in the presence of our God.

Ray Bolz captures a little of the thrill and wonder of the recognition of the crowns of joy on that day in his moving Christian song with the title "Thank You":

"I dreamed I went to heaven;
you were there with me.
We walked upon the streets of gold
beside the crystal sea.
We heard the angels singing, then
someone called your name.
You turned and saw the young man;
he was smiling as he came.

And he said, 'Friend you may not
know me now'.
Then he said, 'But wait!
You used to teach my Sunday school
when I was only eight.
And every week you would say a
prayer before the class would start.
And one day when you said that
prayer, I asked Jesus in my heart.
Thank you for giving to the Lord;
I am a life that was changed.

Thank you for giving to the Lord;
I am so glad you gave!
Then another man stood before you.
He said, 'Remember the time a
missionary came to your church;
His pictures made you cry?
You didn't have much money, but you
gave it anyway.
Jesus took the gift you gave; that's why
I'm here today.
One by one they came, far as the eye
could see.

*Each life somehow touched by your
generosity.
Little things that you had done,
sacrifices made,
Unnoticed on the earth, in heaven now
proclaimed.*

*I know up in heaven you're not
supposed to cry,
But I am almost sure there were tears
in your eyes.
As Jesus took your hand, you stood
before the Lord;
He said, 'My child, look around
you, for great is your reward'!
(Words and music by Ray Bolz, Copyright 1988
by Gaither Music Company)*

CHAPTER 7
Handling A Moral Fog
1 Thessalonians 4:1-12

"Finally, brothers, we instructed you how to live in order to please God, as in fact you are living. Now we ask you and urge you in the Lord Jesus to do this more and more. For you know what instructions we gave you by the authority of the Lord Jesus.

It is God's will that you should be sanctified: that you should avoid sexual immorality; that each of you should learn to control his own body in a way that is holy and honourable, not in passionate lust like the heathen, who do not know God; and that in this matter no one should wrong his brother or take advantage of him. The Lord will punish men for all such sins, as we have already told you and warned you. For God did not call us to be impure, but to live a holy life. Therefore, he who rejects this instruction does not reject man, but God, who gives you his Holy Spirit.

Now about brotherly love we do not need to write to you, for you yourselves have been taught by God to love all the brothers throughout Macedonia. Yet we urge you, brothers, to do so more and more.

Make it your ambition to lead a quiet life, to mind your own business and to work with your hands, just as we told you, so that your daily life may win the respect of outsiders and so that you will not be dependent on anybody."

When men discovered the compass they thought problems of navigation at sea were over. Of course adjustments between magnetic north and true north needed to be taken into consideration. Also, with the use of iron ships the compass needed to be shielded to give an accurate reference point. There is in every person a compass. It is called our conscience, but it is not an accurate guide unless it too is shielded form other influences. This is why it is vital to test your conscience by the true north of this scripture. People say, "Let your conscience be you guide." That could mean disaster. Our conscience needs to be rightly informed and shielded from all effects that can prejudice it.

We have noted how successful is the Church at Thessalonica. It is growing in faith, love and hope. We might say, "Leave them and move on and establish the Gospel elsewhere." This was not Paul's way. His desire is that they will know and do God's will. Many people say to me, "I am trying to find the will of God." If I know them well or think that they can take an enigmatic comment, I will ask, "Has God lost his will then?" There really should be no difficulty in discovering the will of God in broad-brush strokes. "It is God's will that you should be holy" (v.3).

God is more interested in character than career. He is much more interested in who you are than what you do. For every Christian the will of God is "that you should be holy". The word "holy" is one of the most common words in the Bible, and yet it is one of the most misunderstood words in our language. Even Batman's sidekick Robin used the word a lot. Did you hear about the time Batman said, "I don't understand it, Robin, the Batmobile is out of fuel." Robin said, "Holy fuel tank, Batman." Batman said, "Right again, boy wonder."

God has called us to be holy, but how many of us want that word on our résumé? What if I was describing you to someone else and I said, "Kind, friendly, funny, loving . . . and holy." All the other descriptive words have a favourable impact, but not everyone feels good about the word "holy." If someone says you are "holier than thou" or "Holy Joe" or, heaven forbid, a "holy roller" they are not being complimentary. I wonder what the word holy conveys to you. It is dismal to some, who associate it with no jokes, hair shirts and cold showers. It is monastic to others. The mental picture is of stone cells. Nothing could be further from the truth. In the Bible holiness is a practical thing. It is concerned with home, church and community.

We will discover that you cannot be holy by yourself. Holiness is primarily concerned with relationships. Three areas are involved: the relationship between men and women, Christian and Christian, Christian and neighbour. Holiness has to be worked out in marriage, church and work. If you cannot be holy in the every day business of life, a monastery will not help.

God wants me to be holy! Therefore if I live for myself, I am against God's will. Chuck Colson said it well: "Holiness is the everyday business of every Christian. It evidences itself in the decisions we make and the things we do, hour by hour, day by day." *(Charles W. Colson, Loving God, Zondervan Publishing House 1983).*

You may be thinking, "Okay, God is holy, but what does 'holy' mean?" The Hebrew word used in the Old Testament is *kadah* which literally means "to cut apart, separate." The New Testament word is *hagios* which is the same root word for "sanctified" or "consecrated." It basically means "separate, distinct, different."

Four times in this passage Paul refers to moral instruction he gave them when he was with them (v.1,2,6,11). Paul taught them not only the essence of the good news, but also the essence of the good life. He taught them not only the necessity of faith, love and hope in Jesus but also the necessity of good works, without which the authenticity of our discipleship is inevitably called into question. There is a pressing need today, as the culture strays more and more from Christian origins, to take seriously the example of Paul and the other apostles and give plain, candid, down-to-earth moral instruction.

We live in a permissive, relativistic, immoral situation today, it is urgent that we teach Christian morality. It isn't any harder today than it was in the society, in which Paul himself was teaching and writing. Immorality was a way of life in Thessalonica. Women were held in low esteem and the family had little permanence. The pagan temples throughout the city kept a large staff of prostitutes. Worship and fornication were hand in hand. Women were considered things for pleasure. Demosthenes expressed the belief of many: "We keep prostitutes for pleasure; we keep wives for the begetting of children and for the guardianship of our homes." *(William Barclay, The Letters to the Philippians, Colossians and Thessalonians, The Daily Study Bible [Edinburgh: Saint Andrew Press, 1951]).*

Most, men had several wives throughout a lifetime and extramarital sex was not only accepted, but expected. Among the Jews in Thessalonica, divorce was permitted for a multiplicity of absurd reasons. A man could dismiss his wife simply by writing a writ of divorce. The liberal rabbis had a long list of adequate reasons for divorce, all the way from ruining a husband's meal to raising her voice loud enough to be heard by the neighbours. It was a man's world in which women had no rights and little or no status.

This was the culture in which Paul preached the gospel to both Greeks and Jews. The converts from both groups were called back to God's first intention for sex - marriage and the household.

Let's join one of Paul's classes on these matters. The apostle reminds the Thessalonians of the clear instructions he gave on how to live to please God. Notice these are given "by the authority of the Lord Jesus" (v.2). This is not just Paul's advice as a religious leader. These are the words and desires of our Lord Jesus himself. What instructions did Paul urge believers to do "more and more" (v.1)?

THE RELATIONSHIP BETWEEN MEN and WOMEN.

Has it ever struck you that about half the population of the world is female and the other half is male? It is part of God's created order and we must not deny that. Our sexuality is the source of our greatest ecstasies and agonies. The question behind Paul's instruction is straightforward. Is love something you control, or something that controls you? Many popular songs suggest you can't control it. It just happens to you.

So Paul Simon advises:

"You just slip out the back Jack.
Make a new plan Sam.
You don't need to be coy Roy.
Just get yourself free.
Hop on the bus Gus.

118

You don't need to discuss much.
Just drop off the key Lee.
And get yourself free".
(Paul Simons, "Fifty Ways to Leave Your Lover",
for the album Still Crazy After All These Years
[New York: Columbia Records, 1975] Copyright
Paul Simons 1975).

The apostle clearly states that Christianity is totally different. It is love under control. Your control. It is not just falling in love and later falling out of the romantic feeling that has gripped or dazed you. The new viewpoint says, "that you should avoid sexual immorality; that each of you should learn how to control his own body in a way that is holy and honourable, not in passionate lust like the heathen, who do not know God" (v.4,5). Uncontrolled lust whether in or outside marriage is wrong. Make no mistake about it. God is pleased when married partners enjoy a healthy sex life together. He cheers it. And why shouldn't he? He devised it. His Word clearly enunciates that marriage is to be held in honour (Hebrews 13:4). But the warning is clear: If we remove sex from its original, God-given context, it becomes "sexual immorality", "passionate lust", and "impure". If marriage is no more than legalised lust it will break down. You will find another person to use as an object. We have all heard about the sexual demands that are sometimes selfishly made by one married partner of the other, in terms of aggression, violence, or cruelty. And we need to consider what Paul teaches in verses 4-6.

When I marry two people I assume a romantic love. The vows they say are best defined as a commitment of loyalty. "In this matter no one should wrong his brother or take advantage of him" (v.6). Let me put it plainly: There is no room in Christian circles for affairs. It means no adultery; no hanging around the houses of prostitution; no getting involved sexually with anybody else but your mate in marriage. All such behaviour wrongs others. It steals the property of others and destroys their rights. In counselling, we pastors hear seemingly endless stories of damaged families, of children's lives being ruined by the adulterous affairs of their parents. There is enormous misery and heartache that goes along with this passion after adultery and sexual affairs.

God also takes action about this: "The Lord will punish men for all such sins. For God did not call us to be impure, but to live a holy life" (v.6). Rejecting this instruction is rejecting God. God loves this race of ours and so longs to see whole people emerging from it, that he will take drastic action when people violate his will. Silently, invisibly, his judgement falls. Believers and unbelievers alike cannot escape the painful results of wrong choices. That is the law of inevitable consequences. If we choose to sin, there will be evil results. We cannot avoid it. We can be forgiven, but that does not change the evil results. Forgiveness restores the broken relationship and gives us strength to walk on in freedom in the future, but it does not change or eliminate the hurt of the past.

God has called us to holiness. You can't be holy as long as love controls you. You can be holy when you control love.

At this point, Anglican writer and biblical scholar John Stott makes a helpful comment. "For those of us who are single and have therefore been denied the only God-given context for sexual love. What about them? Well, to begin with, we must accept this teaching of God, however hard it may seem, as God's good purpose for us and society. The only God-given context for sexual love is marriage. And we will not become a bundle of frustrations, inhibitions and neuroses if we gladly accept this standard. We will only become so if we rebel against it. We need to say to one another that it is perfectly possible for our sexual energy to be redirected both into affectionate relationships with many people and into loving service for others. There are multitudes of Christian single men and women who have been able to testify that, alongside a natural human loneliness and sometimes acute pain, there can be immense and joyful fulfilment in service for God and fellow human beings."

The Bible has a great deal to say about moral purity. "Blessed are the pure in heart, for they shall see God" (Matthew 5:8). "Flee from sexual immorality. All other sins a man commits are outside his body, but he who sins sexually sins against his own body. Do you not know that your body is a temple of the Holy Spirit, who is in you, whom you have received from God? You are not your own; you were bought at a price. Therefore honour God with your body" (1 Corinthians 6:18-20).

Remember, your life is not primarily about you or your spouse or your happiness or your sexual fulfilment. Your life is about God! Until this thought grips you I doubt if you will have the right kind of life. God intends that every part of your life bring great glory to him. Purity is not primarily about sex, what you do or don't do, what you watch, read or say. Purity is about God! Purity is the personal decision to honour God with your whole being. So many times when we talk about purity, the questions are in terms of dos and don'ts. Can I go here? Is it wrong to see this movie? Should I listen to this music? Those are legitimate questions, but not the main thing. God has a stake in your lifestyle. He has called you to a standard and is honoured when you respond. The big question is not "Do I want this?" or "Would I enjoy this?" or "Do I need this?" but "Will this bring credit to God?" Purity means living so that God's reputation is enhanced by your personal choices.

Purity is worthwhile because the pure in heart see God. They know him deeply, personally, intimately. They have an inner peace that others do not have. They see God and know the comfort of his presence and the joy of his

122

blessing. Purity will cost you a great deal, but it's one investment you will never regret.

That is the first area of holiness Paul teaches, quite uninhibitedly. He does not go up into the clouds. Holiness is down to earth, touching upon mutual attraction. But there is more.

What is holiness?

2. RELATIONSHIPS WITHIN THE CHURCH.

Once again this is utterly practical. Real holiness will have warmth and affection. The proof someone is a Christian is "love one for another" (John 15: 9-17). This is why you can never be holy by yourself. You need other Christians to love and relate to.

How far is my love for my fellow Christian to go? The centre of it must be the local church but then go as far out as possible. Nothing can damage a Church more than unloving attitudes. Paul says: "Now about brotherly love we do not need to write to you, for you yourselves have been taught by God to love each other. And in fact you do love all the brothers throughout Macedonia. Yet we urge you, brothers, to do so more and more" (v.9,10).

Are we more concerned to love than to be loved? Ronald Dunn writes about a stressful time through which he was passing, and how he felt depressed even when he and his family went away on vacation. Depression was like a grey cloud hovering over him as he awoke each morning, waiting to stay with him through each day. Then, it all changed! It was Thursday and the depression had gone. He had no idea what this should be so. Returning home he opened a letter which had arrived in his absence. It was from a friend who was very aware of Ron's troubles. While in prayer, this friend had sensed a leading to help Ron in a wonderful way: "I have asked God to put on my heart as much burden as he can to lighten yours. I want to bear it." That letter was written at 3.00 a.m. on the morning of the very day when Ron felt that the burden had been lifted off his back! *(Don't Just Stand There … Pray Something!, Ronald Dunn, Scripture Foundation (UK) Ltd., 1993 edition, p.87).*

How does God help our love to increase? By putting us into circumstances that almost force us to love. These are opportunities to refrain from being bitter, resentful, sarcastic or critical toward one another.

Christians do not need to be taught how to love one another. Paul's amazing claim is that God through his Holy Spirit teaches us that, "God has poured out his love into our hearts by the Holy Spirit, whom he has given us" (Romans 5:5). If we give that love of the Spirit a welcome, we can manifest love to each other. If we choose to be bitter, then that love will not be manifested, but if we reject the caustic word, the sharp attitude, then we can show kindness, mercy and grace to one another. Thus, the most amazing claim of the Christian faith is that by means of the Holy Spirit, believers have a new capacity to love, which the unbeliever does not possess. That does not mean that we will immediately feel loving. Many people make that mistake. Christians feel the same way non-Christians do. We often feel angry, put upon, resentful and repulsed. Loving people is about the most difficult thing that some of us can do. We can draw upon the grace that God has given us, we can begin to act lovingly. Love is a decision that we make to draw on our Lord's strength. That is why the apostle tells the Thessalonians to love each other and to do so more and more (v.10).

Paul targets another specific area that needs constant attention in order to please God and live a holy life.

3. HOLINESS AND MY COMMUNITY.

Holiness is not a call to come out of the world, but go out into the world. The call to be separate is not geographical. On the last night before the cross Jesus looked towards heaven and prayed: "My prayer is not that you take them out of the world but that you protect them from the evil one" (John 17:15). So many Christians have made the mistake of thinking that to be holy they must get out of the world. Please don't think if you get into a Christian office you could be holy. You may find it more difficult. We have all had inclinations to withdraw. When life gets rough, we say with the psalmist, "O that I had wings like a dove! I would fly away and be at rest" (Psalm 55:6).

We all have escape fantasies. A serious problem for many Christians is that we can arrange our lives so that we are with non-believers as little as possible. We can attend religious functions that we think are 100 percent Christian. We can develop a crypto-Christian language with Christian jokes and passwords. It is possible to go from womb to tomb in a hermetically sealed container decorated with fish stickers. It is possible to abandon our culture to the devil. Are you aware that Moses, Elijah and Jonah all asked to be taken out of the world? God did not grant their requests (Numbers 11:15; 1 Kings 19:4; Jonah 4:3-8). We need to examine our lives to see if we have functionally removed ourselves from the world. Christ prayed that we wouldn't do this. Separation does not necessarily mean isolation. Worldliness does not consist in how many miles a Christian can put between him and a sinner. It is being right in this dirty world but remaining clean. That requires the help of the Holy Spirit because dirt spreads. Shake hands with a dirty hand and your clean hand does not clean up the dirty hand. You need the Holy Spirit working in and through you to stay holy in an unholy world.

When you are rubbing shoulders with the world around you, there are three things that you will need. "Make it your ambition to lead a quiet life, to mind your own business and to work with your hands" (v.11). People who sing their own praises usually do so without accompaniment. Holiness consists in not drawing attention to yourself. It is to be unobtrusive: "Be quiet. Don't be noisy. Lead a quiet life." A holy person minds his own business. He does not interfere with what other people are doing. A Christian's prime concern is not how others work but how he works. Holiness is hard work.

As Christians our work is especially important because it is the primary place we live out our Christian faith outside the family. Being a Christian is very much about going to work!

Consider some Bible statistics on work: Work is mentioned more than 800 times in the Bible, much more often than worship, music, praise and singing.

Jesus appeared 132 times in the New Testament. 123 of those appearances are in the marketplace. Of the 52 parables of Jesus 45 are in a workplace context. Most of Jesus' life was spent as a carpenter.

Why do we work? Whenever people inherit money, or win the lottery, one of the first questions is "Are you going to stop working?" If the answer is a quick "Yes" you know that work is mostly about money. As Christians, we have some bigger answers to the question. We work to be like God. We were created by God and designed to be like him. The more we are like God the happier and more fulfilled we will be. To be like God is eternally worthwhile. God is a worker. Not because he needs the money but because that's the way he is. Work is what God does. Every day we go to work and do a good job we are being like God. God works. We work. We are at our job to make God look good! We represent him. Our primary call is to follow Jesus; our secondary call is the job Jesus has assigned to us.

Think of it this way: Christians work to be like God, glorify God, represent God, fulfil our calling and serve others-and we get paid! Not the other way around. We don't work to get paid and then serve God as a side effect. That way we count our pay cheque to be written on God not on the bank.

Have you noticed in the Bible that job descriptions are important to God? That must be because so many characters in the Bible are identified by the jobs they did. Most of the major and many of the minor biblical characters are identified by occupation. God must care a great deal about the jobs we do. Never think that God doesn't know. Never imagine that God doesn't care. Job descriptions are not all important to God but they are clearly of interest to God. Our job descriptions are important to God but most important is how we do the jobs we have. God doesn't reward on the basis of which job but how we labour. Do we serve out employer but work for the Lord? Maybe some of us need to get a

128

new job. Not a new place of work but a new attitude to the job we do. Whatever your job, consider it your current assignment in God's ministry. Work hard. Work well. Know that you and your job are important. Don't let the world's pecking order peck you down. Never become selfishly proud of your job and never be ashamed of any honourable job you do for God. Find your worth in your relationship to God and the honour of serving on him through it. Trust him for the final outcome.

Balzac once worked for a firm of lawyers. One day he received a note from the office. "You are requested not to come to work today there is a great deal of work to be done." Strange but true. But it should not be written of a true Christian. Charles Lamb has written of, "The dry drudgery of the desks dead wood." There is a tedium in most jobs. My sympathies go out to someone who must endure the mediocre.

How can we solve the problem of drudgery? There is a Bible psychology of "working for the Lord, not for men" (Colossians 3:24). The normal pattern for a Christian is to earn his own living. Not doing so is a sin. The early church had a record second to none of support for those with genuine needs. But they were not to wilfully become dependent on anybody. That would never earn the respect of outsiders.

Here is what holiness is about. Living in a dirty world with clean hands, "so that your daily life may win the respect of outsiders and so that you will not be dependent on anybody." I plead with you not to think of Christian service as something to be done in your leisure time. It is how you function in your daily life.

Jonathan Edwards, one of the great theologians of early American history, once made this resolution: "Resolved, never to do anything, which I should be afraid to do if it were the last hour of my life." *(The works of Jonathan Edwards, revised & corrected by Edward Hickman, Banner Of Truth Trust 1976).*

Sadly, too many people hunger for happiness instead of hungering for holiness. A. W. Tozer wrote: "The emphasis of the New Testament is not upon happiness but holiness. God is more concerned with the state of people's hearts than with the state of their feelings. Go to God and tell Him that it is your desire to be holy at any cost and then ask Him to make you holy whether you are happy or not. Be assured that in the end you will be as happy as you are holy; but for the time being let your whole ambition be to serve God and be Christ-like." *(Of God and Men. A. W. Tozer p.46)*

You have available to you the power that's necessary to solve the real problems of your life. He is Jesus Christ. And once you have the Saviour, you also have the Holy Spirit. You can do all things through him. Holiness is an urgent necessity.

CHAPTER 8
The Dead at His Coming
1 Thessalonians 4:13-18

In 1996, Jeanne Calment was the oldest living human whose age could be verified. On her 120th birthday, she was asked to describe her vision for the future. "Very brief," she said. Another woman was asked the benefits of living to the age of 102. After a pause, she answered, "No peer pressure!"

The apostle Paul has something to say about death we all need to know. I guarantee it can encourage you.

"Brothers, we do not want you to be ignorant about those who fall asleep, or to grieve like the rest of men, who have no hope. We believe that Jesus died and rose again and so we believe that God will bring with Jesus those who have fallen asleep in him. According to the Lord's own word, we tell you that we who are still alive, who are left till the coming of the Lord will certainly not precede those who have fallen asleep. For the Lord himself will come down from heaven, with a loud command, with the voice of the archangel and with the trumpet call of God and the dead in Christ will rise first. After that, we who are still alive and are left will be caught up together with them in the clouds to meet the Lord in the air. And so we will be with the Lord forever. Therefore encourage each other with these words."

The next major world event is the return of the Lord Jesus Christ. There are 1,845 references in the Old Testament alone and a total of 17 books that give it eminence. Of the 260 chapters in the whole New Testament, there are 318 references to Christ's Second Coming. That averages one out of every 30 verses. Furthermore, 23 of the 27 New Testament books refer to the Second Coming. Interestingly, three of these four books are single chapter letters, which were written to specific persons on a single subject. Another interesting factor is that for every prophecy on the first coming of Christ – when he was born as a baby in Bethlehem – there are eight prophecies on Christ's Second Coming.

You cannot really preach the Gospel adequately and ignore this subject. True, the Gospel centres on the cross. There are approximately 300 references to it in scripture. No other event has as many references as the cross and the Second Coming of Christ. Our faith looks back to the cross. Our hope looks forward to his coming. We should live in love right in the middle of these great events. I shall not answer all your questions in this chapter. However, we can discuss some fascinating, comforting and challenging information.

Paul preached the whole Gospel to the Thessalonians. He did not want them ignorant about the future hope of the believer. So excited was Paul that this might happen in his lifetime, he managed to convey that awesome fact. Of course every generation of Christians hope that they will not pass through the process of physical death. We are looking for the up-taker not the undertaker. This was now troubling some believers. They were expecting the Lord to return any day. They felt their loved ones who had died would not be resurrected until the final resurrection at the end of time. They would not see them again until that far-off event. Death leaves the impression that the one who has died is out of things. This was worrying the Thessalonians. It was a natural reaction.

Paul wrote to dispel their ignorance. They are going to get front seats. They will not miss anything. "God will bring with Jesus those who have fallen asleep in him" (4:14). That takes all the fear away. It will be lovely to go straight to Jesus. It will be marvellous not to have to go through the process of death. A Christian can be torn two ways. Like Paul we may say, "I am torn between two: I desire to depart and be with Christ, which is better by far; but it is more necessary for you that I remain in the body" (Philippians 1:23,24). Often it is more necessary for us! There is still much that God must do in us and through us before we say our final good night to the world. If you could see a single Christian in glory you would not want to pull them back into this world. You would envy their position. If you have blessing here, that is nothing to the benefit of eternity. Therefore, the Christian is not allowed the luxury of worldly grief. We are not. "To grieve like the rest of men who have no hope" (4:13).

How miserable the world is about death. A caption on a poster read: "The first two minutes of a man's life are the most critical." Graffiti underneath exclaimed: "The last two are pretty dicey as well."

I doubt that there has been a culture that has spent more money on death or less time and attention to what comes after death. Parents in previous generations would tuck their children in bed at night and have them say a little prayer:

"Now I lay me down to sleep,
I pray the lord my soul to keep.
If I should die before I wake,
I pray the Lord my soul to take."

Isn't that a light-hearted way to send a child off to bed? Did you know there is a second verse?

"Our days begin with trouble,
Our life is but a span.
And cruel death is always near,
So frail a thing is man."

"Good night darling – pleasant dreams!" People taught their child to pray this way because they wanted them to know that death is real, but it is not the end.

How old were you when you began to realise people die?
Jack Kornfield wrote an interesting poem called *"Reverse Living."*

"I think that the life cycle is backwards.
You should die first, get it out of the way.
Then you live in an old-age home.
You are kicked out when you are too young.
You get a gold watch and you go to work.
You work 40 years, until you are young enough to enjoy retirement.
You go to college, you party until you're ready for high school.
You become a little kid, you play, you have no responsibilities.
You become a little boy or a little girl.
You go back to the womb.
You spend your last 9 months floating.
And you finish off as a gleam in someone's eye."
(Jack Kornfield, Source Unknown)

We can't live in reverse. So, we must prepare ourselves for death and what happens after we die.

The story has been told of a man who regularly read the Times Newspaper obituary column and read his own obituary. He phoned the editor, "I have just read my own obituary in you newspaper," he complained. There was a silence before the editor enquired, "Where are you speaking from now?"

The most certain fact of life is death. You can tell a Christian funeral: there may be tears, that is natural - but you know this is not the end. For the Christian it is just an address change. The fact of death is unmentionable in some company because we live in a world without God and without hope. True, we do feel the parting. Death hurts a believer.

Steve Brown writes, "I was speaking at a religious emphasis week at a Christian college. Shortly before I went to speak at the college, a woman I had known for a number of years died. She had been one of Christ's most faithful servants. Her witness had literally touched thousands of people in some exciting and positive ways. Her daughter was a student at the college and one evening after the meeting I noticed her standing in line waiting to speak to me. I was interested in what she was going to say. When she got up to me, she said, 'Mr Brown, I'm Sara Clark (not her name).' 'Sara,' I said, 'I knew your mother and I loved her. She was an inspiration to so many of us. I know this must be a difficult time for you.' 'Not at all', she said smiling. 'I know where my mother is. She is in heaven and her funeral was a witness to how our family is praising God. We saw a number of people come to know Christ at the funeral. Don't waste any pity on me I'm a Christian.'

With uncharacteristic bluntness (well, maybe a little characteristic), I said, "Sara don't give me that kind of balderdash. If your mother's dead and you're happy about that you're not playing with a full deck." Do you know what happened? She fell apart. The tears flowed for the first time in weeks. Sara and I spent a lot of time together that week talking about her mother, how she loved her and how much she missed her. Most of the time I just let her talk and cry and be angry. She had found someone who allowed her not to be 'Christian' for a change, someone who didn't reject her honest feelings. Sara is doing fine now. She still misses her mother. She knows that her mother is with Christ and Sara has a much stronger witness to her friends now because it is honest and free.

The point? Sara had been given a set of standards that as a Christian she felt she must maintain. One of those standards was that Christians praise God all the time and never deal with tragedy honestly lest they hurt their witness for Christ. By allowing people to be human, we give them permission to be free."
(When Being Good Isn't Good Enough, Stephen Brown, Crossway Books 1991).

We feel and we grieve. But we mourn over our own loss. "I'm sorry that you have lost your wife," said a friend to a new widower. "I haven't lost her," he replied, "I know exactly where she is."

Paul dispels ignorance concerning the dead at Christ's coming. For death Paul used the phrase: "those who have fallen asleep" (v.13). That reminds me of the Children Church Teacher who asked her class why it is important to be quiet in church. One bright little girl replied, "Because people are sleeping!" That is not what Paul had in mind, of course. The phrase "fallen asleep" is used to describe believers who have died. The term is never used in the New Testament of anyone but believers. It never says of a non-believer when he died that he "fell asleep". There is a wonderful lesson in that. It shows that death, for the believer, is nothing more than sleep.

When referring to Lazarus who had died, Jesus said, "Our friend Lazarus has fallen asleep; but I am going there to wake him up" (John 11:11). By the way, this word in Greek is where we get our word "cemetery." It was the early Christians' optimistic name for a graveyard because they knew it was a sleeping place, a dormitory for dead people who will one day be resurrected;

Have you ever wondered what it feels like to die? You practise it every night. When you fall asleep you are quietly resting. You expect to wake up again in the same room. One day it will be a place prepared by Jesus (John 14:2,3).

Some people have wrongly taken the apostle's phrase to mean the dead remain in an unconscious state until Jesus returns. I cannot believe that a man so alive as Paul would consider death gain if it was less of the conscious presence of Christ he experienced on earth (Philippians 1:21).

The thing we must remember in dealing with this matter of life beyond death is that when time ends, eternity begins. The Thessalonians, like us today, were projecting the sequence of time into eternity. We all wrestle with the concept of eternity. We tend to think of it as time going on limitlessly; that, as is the case here on earth, we must wait for certain events which are yet future. That is how it will be in heaven, we feel, despite the fact that the word of God seeks to show that time and eternity are two different things.

Dr. Arthur Custance, a Canadian scientist makes a helpful comment on this: "The really important thing to notice is that Time stands in the same relation to Eternity in one sense, as a large number does to infinity. There is one sense in which infinity includes a very large number, yet it is quite fundamentally different and independent of it. By analogy, reduction of Time until it gets smaller and smaller is still not Eternity. Nor do we reach Eternity by an extension of Time to great length. There is no direct pathway between Time and Eternity. They are different categories of experience." *(Doorway Paper No.37, Arthur Custance. Published by the author).*

Augustine understood this. He devoted Book 11 of The Confessions to a discussion of time. He wrote, "What then is time? If no one asks me, I know; if I want to explain it to someone who does ask me, I do not know." When asked, "What was God doing before creation?" he states, "Since God invented time along with the created world, such a question is nonsense and merely betrays the time-bound perspective of the questioner. Before time there is only eternity and eternity of God is never ending present."

Time has sequences: past, present and future. But eternity has only one dimension: it is present, now. We struggle with that, as the Thessalonians also did.

In time I am at a desk in Holsby Brunn, Sweden writing these words. (I am here to teach at a Bible School). In a few days time I will be back at the Good News Broadcasting recording studio to prepare some radio programmes. It will not be long before I fly to America for some preaching engagements. That will be true only of my body. That says nothing about where my mind may be. Minds are not limited to space, or time, or sequence. They can go anywhere and experience anything at any time. Eternity is much more like that. That is why we have great difficulty understanding prophetic passages in scripture in terms of time when they are really eternal events. In eternity there is no past or future, only the present now. Within that now all events will happen.

There probably is sequence of experience in eternity, but it is not based on chronology; it is based upon spiritual readiness. There are scriptural passages that seem to support this. For instance, "The Lamb that was slain from the creation of the world" (Rev.13:8). The cross happened at a particular moment in world history; we can date it. We know when the Lord Jesus Christ was slain as the Lamb of God. Yet scripture says it occurred from the creation of the world. How can you explain how this historical event took place at a certain time on earth, but is said to have occurred before the earth was properly functioning? If you try to project all the thoughts and relationships of time into eternity, you are sure to have real difficulty with this. But if you remember that in eternity all things are present at one time, then of course it is no problem.

Take another example. Paul states, "Praise be to the God and Father of our Lord Jesus Christ, who has blessed us in the heavenly realms with every blessing in Christ. For he chose us in him before the creation of the world" (Ephesians 1:3,4). How do you explain that? Only when you see eternity not as a series of events in a sequence of time, but as relating to us in a different way, can you explain it.

When a believer steps out of time, he is in eternity. The big event of the future is that Jesus is coming again for the believer. Surely it is this event which welcomes every believer the moment he dies. It may be many years before it happened in time. However, this person is no longer in time but eternity. The experience of that believer, does not leave anyone behind. All his loved ones who know Christ are there as well. This includes his Christian descendants who were not born when he died! Since there is no past or future in heaven, this must surely be true. Even those who, in time, stand beside a grave and weep and then go home to an empty house, are in his experience, with him in heaven.

Dr. Custance reasons further, "The experience of each saint is shared by all other saints, by those who have preceded and those who are to follow. For them all, all history, all intervening time between death and the Lord's return is suddenly annihilated so that each one finds to his amazement that Adam, too, is just dying and joining him on his way to meet the Lord: and Abraham and David, Isaiah and the Beloved John, Paul and Augustine, Hudson Taylor and you and I – all in one wonderful experience meeting the Lord in a single instant together, without precedence and without the slightest consciousness of delay, none being late and none too early."*(Dr. Custance, Doorway Paper No. 37 Published by the author).*

I am aware of a problem passage in this connection in Revelation 6: 9-11. John is shown a scene of "The souls of those who had been slain because of the word of God and the testimony they had maintained. They call out in a loud voice, 'How long, Sovereign Lord, holy and true, until you judge the inhabitants of the earth and avenge our blood?' Then each of them was given a white robe and they were told to wait a little longer, until the number of their fellow-servants and brothers who were to be killed as they had been was completed." Does this contradict what I have written? Here are souls in heaven needing to wait for God to avenge them. What is the explanation? I think that this is best understood by the fact that these martyred believers are empathising with the conditions of earth. They are in eternity. They have moved into eternal relationships, but they are concerned about what is happening on earth. On earth there is always the awareness of time, delay and waiting. Since John is still on earth (on the island of Patmos) their expression of concern must be voiced in the language of time.

I believe that Paul knew the difference between time and eternity, but he reassures the Thessalonians, without becoming academic, that the living and the dead will be together when our Lord returns. That is the point at issue. He says, in effect, "Yes, you will see your loved ones immediately when the Lord returns. Whether you join that event when you die or whether the Lord comes while you are yet alive your loved ones will be with him." That is the focus of his thoughts.

Since writing the above lines I have returned from Sweden. I am heading home, which is not far from where John and Charles Wesley had their childhood. It reminds me that many of our great hymns were produced to help the believers die well. Charles Wesley's splendid words: "Happy if with my latest breath I may gasp his name preach him to all and cry in death: Behold! Behold, the Lamb".

You cannot have a more admirable ambition than to die well. Christianity not only teaches you how to live but how to die. If you are in Jesus what happened to Jesus will happen to you. When he died he committed his spirit to the Father and he rose again. We will all be together do not be concerned about that. You will find your loved ones again when the Lord returns.

How will it happen?

You will get confused if you regard the coming of the Lord, as though it were a single event, an immediate and once-for-all appearing. The coming of the Lord is a series of events. This series has a dramatic beginning, as Paul describes here, with Jesus coming to take his living and dead believers to be with him. It has an even more dramatic ending when as Jesus himself said, he would materialise himself to the entire world: "He is coming with the clouds and every eye will see him" (Revelation 1:7). That is a different event from the one here described. You cannot make those fit together. In between them is a period of time during which Jesus is present on the earth though not always visibly so.

When Scripture talks about the coming, (Greek word, *parousia*) it sometimes looks at the beginning of that series, sometimes it looks at the end of it or in-between. The *parousia* of Jesus is a series of events. His first coming lasted around 30 years and included a variety of events. After our Lord's resurrection for 40 days Jesus was here on earth. He appeared to the disciples in Jerusalem and in Galilee. People heard reports that he was around but nobody could find him except when he chose to be seen. That is the same condition that will prevail on earth during this time of the coming of the Lord. If we comprehend that it will help us greatly to grasp what is described.

There are three sounds connected with this initial appearing of Jesus. These sounds affect different groups.

First: the command of the Lord.

"The Lord himself will come down from heaven with a loud command" (v.16). This is a military term that was issued when the troops were "at ease" and it was time for them to "fall in". Who is that cry addressed to? Jesus himself said, "A time is coming and has now come when the dead will hear the voice of the Son of God and those who hear will live" (John 5:25). When Jesus stood before the tomb of Lazarus, he: "called in a loud voice, 'Lazarus come out'"! (John 11.43). To the amazement of the crowd the dead man appeared at the doorway of the

145

tomb. As many commentators have pointed out, if Jesus had not said "Lazarus", he would have emptied the graveyard! Someone once described Jesus as "The world's worst funeral director – he broke up every funeral he ever attended, including his own" *(Dennis Bennett, None O'clock in the Morning, Kingsway).* But the hour is coming when all the dead shall hear the voice of the Son of God and come out! That is what Paul is talking about here. Stanley Spencer has painted a churchyard scene with bodies coming out of their tombs. Some think it grim. Those with eyes to see are excited. The cry of command is addressed to the dead; to those in the tombs who had "fallen asleep in him" (v.14).

The second sound is the voice of the Archangel.

The only angel in the Bible called an archangel is Michael. Though Gabriel is a great angel he is not called an archangel in the Scripture. Michael has a special responsibility towards Israel. An angel said to Daniel, "At that time Michael, the great prince who protects your people, will arise" (Daniel 12:1). "Your people" means Israel. Michael is always connected with Israel. Michael will arise and then there shall be a resurrection. As Jesus comes down with his booming command, Michael's voice is echoing behind him. Those who are in the tombs will come out (Daniel 12:2). Also, the living nation of Israel will be summoned to a new relationship with God. Details of this event concern the 144,000

Israelites, twelve tribes of Israel (see Revelation 7 and 14). These will be called into a fresh relationship with Jesus to follow him wherever he goes on earth during the time of his presence. He is imperceptible to the world but visible to them. That all begins when Jesus returns for his church and the archangel calls Israel into a new relationship with the Lord.

The third sound is the trumpet call of God.

The Bible is filled with references to trumpets and they have a number of different meanings. In Exodus 19 a very loud trumpet was used to call the people out to meet with God. In Zechariah 9:14, a trumpet was used as a signal that the Lord was about to rescue His people. The trumpet sounds forth at the Rapture because God's people are called out in order to be rescued. The world will not hear this call only those to whom it is addressed. Paul pinpoints those in 1 Corinthians 15:51, "We will not all sleep but we will all be changed – in a flash, in the twinkling of an eye, at the last trumpet." What an excellent verse for a Church Crèche, "We will not all sleep but we will all be changed!" But this verse is especially addressed to living believers. We are not all going to die, but we shall all be changed. The biggest Christian meeting ever is coming. No wonder it will be in the air. There is not a stadium on earth that could contain it. Satan is called: "the prince of the air". On that day the air will belong to the believer. This is a statement of priority. That would have calmed the concerns of the Thessalonians. Notice that it is the dead "in Christ" who are raised. This is only a resurrection of believers. The unsaved are left in their graves to be raised at the Great White Throne judgment one thousand years later (see Revelation 20:5).

What a marvellous hope we have.
"Therefore encourage each other with these words" (v.18). This is the ultimate family reunion. Revel in the comfort it brings in old age as the hour of death becomes more a conscious thought.

Few feel encouraged in their late years. The opposite is far more common.

"There are a lot of men who
creep into the world to eat and sleep
and know no reason why they're born
save only to consume the corn,
devour the cattle, bread and fish
and leave behind an empty dish;
and if their tombstones, when they die,
were to flatter or to lie,
there's nothing better can be said
than that they've eaten up their bread,
drunk up their drink and gone to bed."
(Author unknown)

We sing our saddest songs longest if we live and die without a sense of purpose. Unlike the empty condolences of the heathen in the face of death, these words comfort as nothing else can because they overflow with the real hope. Jesus died and rose again. He said that he would meet me on the other side of the grave or if I am still alive at the time, when he comes for his church.

I love the story I heard in a recorded message by Bishop Ken Ulmer, the pastor of a church in Los Angeles, USA. He told about two men who were in an art museum looking at a painting of a chess game. One character looked like a man; the other character looked a lot like the Devil. The man is down to his last piece on the chessboard. The title of the painting is Checkmate. One of the two men looking at this painting was a chess champion, and something about the painting fascinated him. He said to his friend, "Something about this painting bothers me. I want to study it a little longer. You go ahead and wander around."

As he looked more carefully, his head started nodding, and his hands started moving. When his friend returned, he said, "The man who painted this picture must either change the picture or change the title because the King still has one more move.

May I encourage you with these words: *The King still has one more move.*

A teenager named David is up against a mighty, moving mountain of muscle named Goliath. He tried King Saul's armour but disappears into it. He can't even handle an adult sword. It looks like

Checkmate, but – *The King still has one more move.*

Daniel is thrown into a den of lions, because he refuses to stop praying to his God. The lions are hungry. He is in there all night. As dawn breaks, King Darius calls down. He discovers it has become the lions in Daniel's den! Daniel is fine because – *The King still has one more move.*

Moses convinces a nation of oppressed slave to run away from the most powerful man on earth. Pharaoh came after him. They have the Red Sea in front of them and the greatest army of its day behind them. The people say to Moses, "It's all over. We're going to die." Moses says to God, "Over to you" because – *The King has one more move.*

Two people were walking to a village called Emmaus about seven miles away from Jerusalem. Jesus had died and with him their hopes. Jesus himself came up and walked along with them; but they didn't recognise him. By the time the journey was over they knew who he was. Their hearts burned within them. They knew, death had not been cheated but conquered. Because – *The King has one more move.*

"Encourage each other with these words" (v.18).

CHAPTER 9
The Date of His Coming
1 Thessalonians 5:1-11

Chuck Swindoll tells the story of a man who ordered an expensive, extremely sensitive barometer from a respected company. When it arrived, he was disappointed to discover that the needle was stuck on the dial marked "hurricane." After shaking his new gauge several times to no avail, he decided to write a scathing letter to the manufacturer. He mailed the letter the next day on his way to the office. That evening he returned home to find that his barometer was missing – along with his house which had been hurled away by a hurricane!

The Bible is our barometer. B.I.B.L.E. - **B**asic **I**nformation **B**efore **L**eaving **E**arth. The verses we are considering now point to a holy hurricane.

"Now brothers, about times and dates we do not need to write to you, for you know very well that the day of the Lord will come like a thief in the night. While people are saying, "Peace and safety", destruction will come on them suddenly, as labour pains on a pregnant woman and they will not escape.

But you, brothers, are not in darkness so that this day should surprise you like a thief. You are sons of the light and sons of the day. We do not belong to the night or to the darkness. So then, let us not be like others who are asleep, but let us be alert and self-controlled. For those who sleep, sleep at night and those who get drunk, get drunk at night. But since we belong to the day, let us be self-controlled, putting on faith and love as a breastplate, and the hope of salvation as a helmet. For God did not appoint us to suffer wrath but to receive salvation through our Lord Jesus Christ. He died for us so that, whether we are awake or asleep, we may live together with him. Therefore encourage one another and build each other up, just as in fact you are doing."

Paul is coming to grips with the question of the time of the Lord's return. All of us seem to want a date to circle on the calendar but Paul had taught the Thessalonians that they would not know the date exactly.

This is the first mention in the letter of the phrase "the day of the Lord" (v.2). As we have previously noted, it is important to understand that it is not just a single 24 hour day but an elastic and extended length of time. When someone says, "We live in the day of high tech. communication," they are not talking about one single day, but a period of time which covers a number of events over a period – probably seven years, the whole period being called the *parousia* or presence of Christ. When Christ returns he will remain on earth for this time. Thus, the "day of the Lord" is a series of events perhaps even extended into the millennium, the thousand-year reign of Christ that follows. Actually the phrase, "day of the Lord" refers to any period of time when God acts directly and clearly in human affairs. It may be in blessing, as in the pouring out of the Holy Spirit on the day of Pentecost, or it may be in judgement. It may be that the same event will be a judgment to some people and a blessing to others.

In this case, says Paul, "About times and dates we do not need to write to you" (v.1). That is also what Jesus had said. In that period of time when he was risen from the dead and appearing with his disciples on occasion and then disappearing again, during one of these appearances they asked him, "Lord are you at this time going to restore the kingdom to Israel?" (Acts 1:6). They were asking, "Is this the time when you will fulfil the predictions of the prophets that Israel will be the chief of the nations and the Messiah will reign personally upon the earth?" Here is the Lord's remarkable answer to their question: "It is not for you to know the times or dates the Father has set by his own authority" (Acts 1:7). Only the Father knew the answer to their question. Then Jesus went on to outline to them the programme that would affect them: "But you will receive power when the Holy Spirit comes on you; and you will be my witnesses in Jerusalem and in all Judea and Samaria and to the ends of the earth" (Acts 1:8).

We must understand that though we cannot name the definite date when the Lord will appear and begin the "day of the Lord", there are three characteristics of that day that we can look for and understand.

1. GOD'S DAY WILL BE UNEXPECTED

"The day of the Lord will come like a thief in the night" (5:2). A thief does not want to draw attention to himself, he enters silently and does his work. God will have his day. (Read Amos 5:18ff; Joel 2:1ff; Zephaniah 1:14-18; and Isaiah 2:12-21 for a description of this period).

Another term for this period is "the time of Jacob's trouble" (Jeremiah 30:7). Many prophetic students also call it the *Tribulation* and point to Revelation chapter 6 to 19 as the Scripture that descriptively expounds this event.

When Jesus spoke about his future return in Luke 17:20-37, it is the note of the unexpected that he emphasises. We will not get side-tracked from what Paul says if we consider it in the context of what Jesus had taught.

Once, having been asked by the Pharisees when the kingdom of God would come, Jesus replied, "The kingdom of God does not come with your careful observation, nor will people say, 'Here it is,' or 'There it is,' because the kingdom of God is within you."

Then he said to his disciples, "The time is coming when you will long to see one of the days of the Son of Man, but you will not see it. Men will tell you, 'There he is!' or 'Here he is!' Do not go running off after them. For the Son of Man in his day will be like the lightning, which flashes and lights up the sky from one end to the other. But first he must suffer many things and be rejected by this generation.

"Just as it was in the days of Noah, so also will it be in the days of the Son of Man. People were eating, drinking, marrying and being given in marriage up to the day Noah entered the ark. Then the flood came and destroyed them all.
"It was the same in the days of Lot. People were eating and drinking, buying and selling, planting and building. But the day Lot left Sodom, fire and sulphur rained down from heaven and destroyed them all.
"It will be just like this on the day the Son of Man is revealed. On that day no-one who is on the roof of his house, with his goods inside, should go down to get them. Likewise, no-one in the field should go back for anything. Remember Lot's wife! Whoever tries to keep his life will lose it, and whoever loses his life will preserve it. I tell you, on that night two people will be in one bed; one will be taken and the other left. Two women will be grinding grain together; one will be taken and the other left." "Where, Lord?" they asked. He replied, "Where there is a dead body, there the vultures will gather."

Notice five key insights about the future.

First: The Now And Then.

The Pharisees assumed the kingdom of God would be a military kingdom. They anticipated that their Messiah would come and return them to the kind of kingdom they enjoyed with David a thousand years earlier. But Jesus said, "The kingdom of God is within you" (17:21). The word translated "within" can also be translated "among." God's kingdom reign is established in the life of a believer, but I think Jesus was saying something more. The kingdom of God was right among them. As Jesus spoke those words to the Pharisees, they didn't want to see that the King was standing right in from of them.

When you think of the "kingdom of God", think of a King. All you need for a kingdom is to have a king. When Jesus rules over your life, you are in his Kingdom. Paul writes that the kingdom of God is "righteousness, peace, and joy in the Holy Spirit" (Romans 14:17). That is personal.

But the kingdom of God has a duel meaning. In addition to being an invisible, personal kingdom in your life, it also has a future aspect. There will be a literal, visible kingdom of God in the future. When Gabriel announced to Mary that she would give birth to a son he made several announcements. He was to be named Jesus, he will be great, and that he would reign for ever. That hasn't happened yet. But one day it will happen.

Second: Lightning In The Sky.

Jesus used metaphors easy to understand, such as lightning. He said that his coming would be "like the lightning, which flashes and lights up the sky from one end to the other" (17:24). How is his coming again like lightning?

First, lightning strikes in a storm. When Jesus returns he will come into a stormy chaotic world.

Second, lightning occurs suddenly. It doesn't slowly meander down. It strikes as fast as . . . er, lightning. It usually travels from cloud to ground and ten flashes back upward at a speed of 1/10,000 of a second. When Jesus comes for his church, he will stop in the clouds and then we will be caught up to meet him, as fast as lightning.

Third, lightning possesses phenomenal power. In the split-second lightning flashes, the air in its channel is heated to incredible temperatures. This rapid heating creates such a shock, there is an audible sonic wave we call thunder. The energy discharged in a single stroke of lightning is enough to lift a family sized car 62 miles straight upward. Amazing power! When Jesus comes, he will not be floating down on a little white puff! He came the first time to save from sin. When he comes again he will be the mighty Lion of the Tribe of Judah!

Fourth, you never know when lightning will strike. We take precautions to avoid it but we never know when it will strike. Back to 1 Thessalonians 5 for a moment. The return of Jesus will be unexpected (v.2). Every time you read of a burglary, or you see lightning flash across the sky, it should serve to remind us to be ready for the return of Christ.

Third: Noah And Lot.

We cannot know the exact date for Christ's return, but it is possible to discern the general time. "Just as it was in the days of Noah, so also will it be in the days of the Son of Man. People were eating, drinking, marrying and being given in marriage up to the day Noah entered the ark. Then the flood came and destroyed them all" (17:26,27). Normal activities and suddenly a family is removed from the earth. Jesus did not stop there. He went on to say, "It was the same in the days of Lot. People were eating and drinking, buying and selling, planting and building. But the day Lot left Sodom, fire and sulphur rained down from heaven and destroyed them all" (17:28, 29).

Notice how clearly in the example Paul uses, that there is a quiet disappearance of the family of God first. Like a thief at work, mutely and furtively, the treasure is taken away. Then the judgment comes (v.2,4).

158

But please notice that it is not all doom and gloom. Yes, there was a flood, but God delivered Noah and his family. Yes, Sodom and Gomorrah were destroyed by fire and sulphur, but God delivered Lot and his two daughters.

Fourth: Mrs. Lot's Mistake.

Jesus said, "Remember Lot's wife!" (17:32). As they were fleeing Sodom, Lot's wife looked back and was ionised. Why did Jesus warn us to remember her? I'm sure Mrs. Lot was basically a good person (the salt of the earth). Her mistake was she couldn't resist one last look. Before Lot moved to Sodom there is no mention of him being married, so we assume he found a wife in Sodom and lived there long enough to have a family. Mrs. Lot married a righteous man and probably accepted his religion and prayed to the One God. She had a 'lean-to' religion. She never fully got over her love for Sodom. On the mountain that day, she was out of Sodom, but Sodom was not out of her. Mrs. Lot represents people who have a superficial interest in God and the Bible, but they never truly involve themselves with Christ.

Mrs. Lot is a sad reminder of how people will be separated. Jesus adds these words: "I tell you, on that night two people will be in one bed, one will be taken and the other left. Two women will be grinding grain together, one will be taken and the other left" (17:34,35). In Revelation 3:3 and 16:15, he used this image to warn believers to watch out. This indicates a selective taking away which happens all over the earth at once. When it is day-time at one place and night-time at another, one will be taken; others will be left.

Fifth: The Vultures Gather.

In the last verse of Luke 17 Jesus answered a final question. His disciples asked him, "Where, Lord?" Notice they did not ask "when?" Jesus replied, "Where there is a dead body, there the vultures will gather" (v.37). Vultures eat dead animals. When they find a dead or dying animal, they fly around in circles before descending to have their meal.

Jesus was answering the question, "Where?" Isn't it obvious what he meant by reply? "Just look where the vultures are circling, and that's where the action will take place." Could the world focus on the Middle East and particularly Israel be the sign of where events will climax when Christ returns?

Let's return to 1 Thessalonians. Scripture clearly teaches that the day of the Lord begins with the removal of God's people; then judgment breaks out on the earth.

Not only will that day be *unexpected.*

IT WILL BE UNMITIGATED.

"While people are saying, 'Peace and safely',

destruction will come on them suddenly", says Paul (5:3). In Matthew 24:21, Jesus said: "Then there will be great distress, unequalled from the beginning of the world until now – and never to be equalled again." We don't like to think about this but to do so is to face reality. In the 260 chapters of the New Testament God reminds us 234 times of the reality of this hopeless world, nearly one verse for every chapter of the New Testament. If life's road was 260 miles long and you saw 234 sign-boards that warned: "This road leads away from God into the dark night of great distress." If you did not turn around and go the other way, you could never place the blame on the one who put the sign on the highway. God has put the signs on the highway all through the New Testament. This *unexpected*, *unmitigated* day has a further dimension to it.

IT IS UNAVOIDABLE.

"Destruction will come on them suddenly, as labour on a pregnant woman and they will not escape" (v.3). The birth of a child cannot be delayed. This metaphor is exciting to contemplate. But I do wonder why he utilised a positive image to follow the negative one of the thief in the night. A thief is a fearsome intruder, a child is a welcome gift. Could it be that for those who do not know Christ the end is like a thief and for a believer it is a new birth. For us who are in Christ the end times will not be death throes but birth pains of a new stage of our eternal life. Whether at the end of our physical life or at the return of Christ, the end will be graduation to heaven. We need not fall into fatalism or despair over the end of the world. It will be like a birth to a new level of existence more sublime than we can imagine.

But the world cannot escape the terrible judgment of God. The only way is provided in Jesus Christ our Lord. It is very important that we understand that God's delay of this event is to give people the chance to see what is happening in their lives and to choose the redemption that is in Christ. 1Thessalonians 5:1-3 emphasises God's judgment on those who do not know Christ. But verses 4-10 emphasises that God will deliver from judgment those who are his children.

As we observe what is coming in world affairs there should be a result in our lives. Paul gives some down-to-earth advice on how to live in this present day.

BE DIFFERENT

Because we know in general terms what will happen this coming day should not surprise us like a thief. "You are all sons of the light and sons of the day. We do not belong to the night or to the darkness." Notice that Paul says, "You are all." There really are no categories of Christians. If you know Jesus you are in the light (see Colossians 1:13). Since we have a special identity we have a significant responsibility. We should live differently. Actually, not only should we be different, we can and we must be. Our conduct demonstrates our condition. Our identity gives us the power to be who we were created to be.

Notice that Paul does not say, "Please be day people." He says, "You are day people, now live like it" (see v.5). In a sermon on this passage, John MacArthur states: "Night people can only be night people, they can't be day people. Night people cannot do the deeds of the day. But day people can do the deeds of the night. We can reach back to old patterns of conduct. But we don't have to because it's not consistent with our new nature and our new identity and our sphere of life . . . there's no place for night life among day people . . . if you do the deeds of darkness . . . you're going contrary to your nature, you're violating your identity. Our behaviour should be consistent with our nature." *(John MacArthur. 'Night People/Day People,' part 2, GC 52-53)*

Our identity is that we are people of the day. Our responsibility is to act like who we are.

BE DISCIPLINED

"So then, let us not be like others who are asleep...." (v.6). That is a great word for a Sunday service! But what Paul means by that is not only to keep awake in church but do not begin to dream like the world around is dreaming. Do not fall into fantasies such as – the purpose of living is to try to gain wealth or fame. The purpose of life is to use your abilities and your time to fulfil the will of God; to find the adventure, excitement and drama of that instead of wasting time in self-indulgence.

Paul is not saying we must look as though we have been baptised in embalming fluid, grim and humourless. He is urging that we take life seriously. Do not spend time amusing yourself constantly. As the apostle puts it to the Ephesians, "Making the most of every opportunity, because the days are evil" (Ephesians 5:16). Paul is not talking about the duration of time, but rather 'strategic time', the opportunity that God brings our way each day. Like a yacht taking advantage of the wind and the tide to arrive at its planned destination, so we must learn to take each opportunity that God gives.

The most valuable commodity you have to give is time. You can make more money but you cannot make more time. You have exactly the same amount of time each day as every other person on earth: twenty four hours, 1,440 minutes, 864,000 seconds – no more no less. Where you spend time and with whom you spend your time tells a lot about your priorities.

We live in at a time when many people are frantically fighting the clock. They live under the constant stress of juggling time between their

jobs, their families, and the many other various demands. Someone aptly observed:
"Ours is the age of the half-read page,
The quick hash and the mad dash;
The bright nights with the nerves tight;
The plane hop with a brief stop;
The lamp tan in a short span;
The brain strain and the heart pain;
The catnaps till the spring snaps;
And then the fun's done."

The Aberdeen Bestiary is a collection of writings from North England dating back to the 1200s. These allegorical stories about animals are purported to have come from an ancient Greek writer Physiologus. In addition to the dozens of articles about animals there is a fascinating section which describes the six stages of a person's life. I like these age divisions better than some we use today. The Aberdeen Bestiary says stage one is:

(1) Infancy – birth to age 7;
(2) Childhood – 8-14. No surprise so far, but they considered
(3) Adolescence to cover the ages of 14 all the way to age 28. That's why some of you young adults are still having problems: you are still in your adolescence!
(4) Youth was considered to be the ages of 29 to 50! The next stage was called
(5) Maturity, which covered the ages 51 to 69.

(6) Old age started at 70 and was called the riper years when a person enjoys the fruits of their labour.

Whether you are two or ninety-two the study of God's prophetic programme is always meant to have a purifying effect on his people (see 1 John 3:2,3).

Can you imagine anything worse than to be drunk when Jesus comes again? (v.7). Keep your heart by: "putting on faith and love as a breastplate" (v.8). Keep your head by putting on: "the hope of salvation as a helmet" (v.8). You need not fear the return of Christ: "God did not appoint us to suffer wrath but to receive salvation through our Lord Jesus Christ" (v.9).

Be *different* and *disciplined*.

BE DISSEMINATING

"He died for us so that, whether we are awake or asleep, we may live together with him. Therefore encourage one another and build each other up" (v.10,11). To "encourage" means to come alongside someone and give him or her whatever help they need. The phrase "build each other up" was used when someone constructed a house. Every believer around you is undergoing a spiritual construction project. God wants to use you just like the Holy Spirit is used in your life to come alongside and be there for them. The word "encouragement" is mentioned 46 times in the New Testament because God wants us to look for ways to delight in each other.

It is so easy to lose sight of God's perspective. If you enjoy the children's stories of Winnie the Pooh, you know that Pooh's favourite pastime is to put his head in the honey jar. This is a beautiful analogy. Unless we're somewhat different to most people we all enjoy sweet things. Solomon writes, "Pleasant words are a honeycomb, sweet to the soul and healing to the bones" (Proverbs 16:24). To what extent are you using words to build each other up? Flatter me and possibly I will not believe you. Criticise me and perhaps it will be hard for me to like you. Ignore me, and I may struggle with rejection. Encourage me, and I will not forget you. Think about your use of words. Think of someone discouraged or anxious, physically ill, always giving out, lonely or spiritually drifting. What can you say to encourage this person? How will you say it?

I cannot finish this chapter without asking, Are you ready for Christ's return? Have you received salvation through our Lord Jesus Christ? Do you have that assurance? If not, receive him today and you need never fear the Day of the Lord. Why not live today as if it were the last day of your life? What would you settle in your relationship with the Lord?

CHAPTER 10
Getting It All Together
1 Thessalonians 5:12-22

"Now we ask you, brothers, to respect those who work hard among you, who are over you in the Lord and who admonish you. Hold them in the highest regard in love because of their work. Live in peace with each other. And we urge you, brothers, warn those who are idle, encourage the timid, help the weak, be patient with everyone. Make sure that nobody pays back wrong for wrong, but always try to be kind to each other and to everyone else.
Be joyful always; pray continually; give thanks in all circumstance, for this is God's will for you in Christ Jesus.
Do not put out the Spirit's fire; do not treat prophecies with contempt. Test everything. Hold on to the good. Avoid every kind of evil".

"The most important thing in learning to relate to others is personal honesty," said one man and added, "Once you learn to *fake* that, everything else is easy!" Many people, unfortunately, seem to follow that philosophy. One of the most discouraging aspects of modern-day living is the lack of integrity. The children in a prominent family wanted to give their father a special birthday present. They decided to compile a book on the family history. They commissioned a professional biographer. "We have one big problem," they explained. "Uncle George was the black sheep of the family and was sent to the electric chair. These details will spoil the book." "No problem," said the biographer, "I will write that he occupied a chair of applied electronics at an important government institute. He was attached to his position by the strongest ties, and his death came as a real shock!"

I do not understand what has happened to the Christian community. Believers who go regularly to church and profess to believe the Bible often seem to go along with the practices of the world around them with hardly any consciousness that what they are doing is unbiblical and really wrong. They lie without hesitation. They evade paying their bills. They cheat on their taxes. They ignore needy people. They fail to keep appointments. They lose their tempers. They grow critical and caustic. They desert their mates. If the apostle Paul were here he would be very concerned about this. To him the mark of true Christian faith is that everything changes. It affects every area of life. A Christian may no longer act as they did before they came to Christ. This is very clear in the letters the apostle wrote. Every letter ends with pointed, practical applications to daily situations of the truth that he set out.

The letter of 1 Thessalonians is no exception. The closing verses are wonderfully practical guidelines. They help us to get things together in three areas of life.

First, our relationship with *spiritual leaders.*
Second, our relationship with *one another.*
Third, our relationship with *God.*

RELATIONSHIPS WITH SPIRITUAL LEADERS

How should you act toward the leadership of the church? Biblically we don't choose spiritual leaders, we recognise the ones that God sets apart. There are two things which Church members must do with regards to its leaders:

First, Respect Them.

The word means, know them, recognise them, be aware of them, do not take them for granted. I know of churches where pastors are treated as hired servants. Get to know your leader. Understand that they are people and do not ignore them.

Second, Value Them.

"Hold them in the highest regard in love because of their work" (v.13). They have their own idiosyncrasies, we all have those, but they do important work. Christian leaders make mistakes. It is easy to throw stones. There are people who become so angry they try to harm the reputation of a leader with false accusations.

Paul gives three reasons for this care of leaders.

(1) Leaders are sent by the Lord.

Paul says: "respect those who work hard among you, who are over you in the Lord" (v.12). Regardless of the human process of appointment, they are God-placed. That does not mean that they cannot go somewhere else. But we must regard them as God appointed.

(2) Leaders are sent to admonish you.

The word "admonish" (v.12), is literally, to put in mind. They remind you of truth that is easily forgotten. They speak against the spirit of the age, the self-centred attitude of the day.

Franklin D Roosevelt said, "An idealist is a man with both feet planted firmly in the air." Church leaders are there to help us keep our feet on the right path.

(3) Leaders work hard.

They spend hours toiling in difficult and sometimes frustrating work. Contrary to what some people think, they do not work a one-day week. The ministry is a very demanding job.

A man once told me, "I'm going to take you out sometime and show you the 'real world'." I wanted to wipe the silly grin off his face, but I didn't. After all, I was a pastor and pastors don't do that sort of thing. But I did tell him, "I see more of the real world in one week than you will see in a lifetime. If you want to see 'the real world' come with me for a while and you'll be glad to get back to the plastic world you call real." I see a lot of the real world and to be honest with you, I don't like much of what I see. The range of problems confronting a spiritual leader in the course of a week is staggering. Respect and value your leader.

RELATIONSHIPS WITH ONE ANOTHER.

What about our behaviour toward one another? Paul's use of the word "brothers" throughout the letter and especially in this passage, indicates that he is speaking to the entire church family. The health of our church depends to a large degree on the commitment not only of the leaders, but also of each one of us to certain standards of conduct.

First: "Live in peace with each other" (v.13).

A deliberate refusal to create factions or to play favourites. I love what Joseph said to his brothers when he sent them back to Israel to get his father and their families. It is very interesting. He wanted to make sure that they did not allow discord to rip them apart when they now had the opportunity to come together again as a family. "As they were leaving, he said to them, 'Don't quarrel on the way!'" (Genesis 45:24). To promote peace we must be proactive about it. "Make every effort to keep the unity of the Spirit through the bond of peace" (Ephesians 4:3).

A peaceful church is a *powerful* church. God needs an arena in which to work. He can't trust some churches with power because they will not become Team Jesus. A peaceful church is a *purposeful* church. If all our energy is concentrated on relational conflict, we have little energy left over for kingdom business. A peaceful church is a *pleasant* church. "How good and pleasant it is when brothers live together in unity" (Psalm 133:1). To be attractive requires unity.

What can we do to help this along? A Church Minister was having trouble with his leadership team. On his way home from a meeting in his frustration he kicked a drink can. Out popped a genie (yes, it's one of those jokes but there is a serious point). The genie thanked the minister for releasing him and offered him one wish (he was just a junior genie and couldn't provide three wishes just yet!) "Thank you," said the Minister, "I wish for an end of all war." The genie said, "That's beyond me, I'm not that influential, try again." "Well," said the Minister, "please make the Church leadership team work well together." The genie thought for a moment, and then said, "Could we go back to your original wish?"

We can 'burn' each other out. The popular areas are music, style of worship and teaching, youth work, the building, the leadership style. What can we do about it? I prepared a paper for a Good News Broadcasting Conference in India which included my research on music, past, present and possible future trends. This may be of interest and help to you. Rather than including it in this chapter I will give it to you as a footnote.

Remember to what you belong. The Church of Christ. We must 'own' the church even the negative bits. But please get real. There will be points of disagreement. If you don't get irritated by something you are probably clinically dead. As someone has commented, "You don't have problems with people buried in a cemetery." Some of the conflict issues are because of life and growth. Don't say, "I'm here as long as I like it." God has called us to relationships that are deeper than that. We must learn to live with difficult people. Have you heard of the railway company that discovered its problems were with the last carriage, so they decided to remove them! If difficult people leave a church they will soon be replaced with other equally difficult people. I meet people who say, "I attend this Church." The church is a family. You don't attend a family, you are part of it. Let's get real. Our unity is not based on perfect agreement. Any time you find perfect agreement you are probably looking at a cult.

Stay focused on what God wants. God has a big picture for us. Satan has a little picture. What is the little picture we focus on? In one Church it was standing too long for worship. There is a simple answer – sit down! Do you know one of the greatest miracles in the Book of Acts? It is when Jews welcomed Gentiles into the Church (see Acts 15). The barriers between them were huge. They got the big picture. What I am trying to say, with feeling because I have been a Church Pastor, let's grow up.

You may say, "But I am trying to live in peace with someone and it's just not working." Here is a verse for you: "If it is possible as far as it depends on you, live at peace with everyone" (Romans 12:18). Are you doing all that you can? If so, two things are going to happen. First, peace becomes possible when you offer it and they accept it. If that is the case, everything is great. Second, peace is impossible when you offer and they refuse. You cannot find peace by trying to please everyone.

Listen (I'm putting my 'former pastor badge' on again). There are some people you will not get on with. You must do all that you can on your side. It may not work because you will get enemies from your position or disposition. What you believe may not be acceptable to them. But you do not need to be hateful. Some people don't like me. I find that hard to understand because I'm a likeable person (I would think that wouldn't I?) I am not going to change what I believe is a biblical position regarding ethical issues. But I must try to be kind.

Who is that person that you're not living in peace with right now? Do you feel guilty? Have you done everything than can to live in peace? Then you are free. And this is something I have looked forward to writing. Get out of God's way. When you have to deal with mean people, the best thing is to let God deal with them. "Do not take revenge my friends, but leave room for God's wrath. For it is written, [now this is what God says] 'it is mine to avenge. I will repay'" (Romans 12:19). Trying to pay-back yourself gets in God's way. Leave room for him to do something. You must understand that God repays evil. If you are reading this and thinking, "Good on you God. Go after him God." Here is another verse for you: "Do not gloat when your enemy falls. When he stumbles, do not let your heart rejoice" (Proverbs 24:17). If you do, it says the Lord will see and disapprove. "But he shouldn't get away with it. This has been going on a long time." All I can write is that God is not finished yet. Get out of his way. He will reward endurance when you endure insults. Has anybody unloaded on you verbally? Just keep walking with God. When a dog barks at a 'Parade', it doesn't stop the show.

Kill your enemies. Really? Yes! But with kindness. You knew there would be a catch didn't you? "If you enemy is hungry, feed him," do the unexpected. "If he is thirsty, give him something to drink." They don't expect that. It just blows them away. It's like heaping "burning coals on his head" (Romans 12:20). A picture of a penitent off to worship intending to add a coal to the altar fire. You may even shame the person by your attitude. Your goal with mean people is not to burn them but to bless them. They may not say, "Well, I'm just burning with shame." But it does affect them.

I like the way Booker T. Washington put this: "I will not allow any man to make me lower myself by hating him. The only way I can destroy my enemy is to make him my friend." Your goal is to treat others the way God has treated you. You were once an enemy of God, alienated from him. Living at peace with him was undeserved. God is simply saying that we are to treat other people in the same way.

Second: "Warn those who are idle" (v.14).

The word is literally the disorderly. Those out of step with the rest of the church family. In Thessalonica it meant those people whom he referred to earlier who had quit their jobs and were waiting for the return of Christ. The word "idle" occurs only here in the New Testament. It was used of a soldier who had stepped out of the ranks and had become disorderly. These spiritual draft dodgers had become undisciplined and disruptive. Our English word "slacker" probably best captures the idea of the Greek word. "Urge them" says the apostle, "tell them to mend their ways." He does not mean to do this in a mean-spirited way. But their behaviour is unacceptable. It is not easy to sit down with a believer and say, "I care about you but the way you are living is out of step with what God expects from you." Resist the urge to gossip about someone. Instead, ask God for the courage, wisdom and love that talks with him or her.

Third: "Encourage the timid" (v.14)

Literally the small-souled person. One who feels inadequate and ungifted. The introverts among us. If the wayward are the *"won't do"* of the church, the timid are the *"want to."* Instead of living on the edge, the timid are huddled in the middle. For every negative statement people need at least five or six positive statements to balance it out. This is addressed to everybody. People who feel out of it, who think they do not belong and cannot contribute anything must be helped to find their place because they do have a place. In the wonderful picture of the body at work, the apostle says. "If the ear should say, 'Because I am not an eye, I do not belong to the body', it would not for that reason cease to be part of the body" (1 Corinthians 12:16). There are people who feel that way. They think, "I cannot do anything. I do not have any gifts." That is wrong thinking. God has equipped all his people with gifts. We are to help each other find our place. Give them something to do and encourage them in the work that they are doing. I love the way Jesus looked for ways to fan into flame the fire that once burned bright (see Matthew 12:20). Isaiah 35:3 and 4 is a great description of how we can encourage the timid: "Strengthen the feeble hands, steady the knees that give way; say to those with fearful hearts, 'Be strong, do not fear, your god will come'."

Fourth: "Help the weak" (v.14)

If the wayward are the "won't do" and the timid are the "want to," then the weak are the "can't do." This means especially those who have difficulty living the Christian life. Perhaps they are not sure of their salvation, or they feel guilty about the past and do not sense they have really been forgiven yet by God. Whatever it may be, the word is to help them, to hold them fast. That demands a little extra effort; a phone call perhaps, an invitation to your home. This is addressed to us all.

Three special attitudes are required for this. First "be patient with everyone"; Second "make sure that nobody pays back wrong for wrong"; Third "always try to be kind to each other and to everyone else" (v.14,15).

Patience is willingness to keep trying over and over again. Some of us have the patience of a hand grenade with the pin drawn. Non-retaliation means that you do not strike back and try to get even with someone who may have hurt you in the process of helping him or her. Helpfulness is a continual attempt to better a situation, to be part of the solution and not part of the problem.

RELATIONSHIP WITH GOD.

What is your attitude to be toward God? In the circumstances where he puts you, "be joyful always" (v.16). The word perhaps ought to be translated, "Be cheerful". Do not let things get you down. Society is filled with despair and gloom. The pressure under which we live today can do this.

A magazine pin-points some telltale signs of stress. It is light-hearted but there is a sting in the tail. "You sleep like a baby: you wake up every two hours crying. You start biting other people's finger-nails. Leisure time is stopping at traffic lights. *(Pressure Points, Peter Meadows, Kingsway Publications 1993).*

But a Christian has an inner resource. Therefore we can obey the word of James, "Consider it pure joy, my brothers, whenever you face trials of many kinds" (James 1:2). Do not take it as an attack upon you. Do not moan and groan and say, "What have I done to deserve this sort of thing?" But rejoice, because it is good for you. Trials make you grow up, make you face yourself and learn things about yourself you did not know. That is why James goes on to say, "That you may be mature and complete, not lacking anything." Many can testify to this.

Paul adds, "Pray continually" (v.17). That is a method of drawing on the inner strength that God provides. I've always had the conviction in administration that if two people are doing the same job in an organisation, one of them is unnecessary. The same would be true of our relationship to God. If he and I are trying to do the task of running the universe, I am duplicating his responsibility. My job description as a Christian is to pray constantly, discover God's will and be implemented by obediently following orders. When I get out of line and assume God's role, I take onto myself authority which is not mine. Added to that, I don't have the wisdom to tackle that job! I was never meant to. I play God when I do.

Have your props been taken away and have you begun to learn that God himself can meet your needs? As you poured out your heart in prayer, sometimes in almost desperate prayer, you discovered that he had quiet ways of answering that taught you that he is enough, the God who can meet your needs. When you are under pressure lean on that inner strength. Let the sign you see on some doors be a reminder: "Push" – P.U.S.H. **Pray Until Something Happens.** Pray continually.

"Give thanks in all circumstances" (v. 18). Why be thankful? Because when you are faced with a trial you are being given an opportunity to glorify God. If you never face pressures, how could anyone ever see that you have an invisible means of support. When the early Christian leaders were arrested by the Sanhedrin, they were beaten for their faith, but they left the Council rejoicing that they had been counted worthy to bear suffering for His name's sake. That is a thoroughly Christian attitude and that is how we ought to face trials.

Notice how Paul underlines this: "For this is God's will for you in Christ Jesus " (v.18). The will of God is not to make some dramatic display of power or gift that is going to attract attention. It is the quiet response you make to the daily trials and circumstances in which you find yourself.

Twice in this letter we have had this phrase, "This is God's will for you." We had it in 4:3, "It is God's will that you should be holy; that you should avoid sexual immorality; that each of you should learn to control his own body." That is the will of God for your *body!* Here is the will of God for your *spirit,* your inner life: "give thanks in all circumstances." If you want to do the will of God there are the two areas clearly set out. Moral purity for your body; continual thanksgiving for your spirit.

How should you react toward the guidance God gives you?

There are two ways: "Do not put out the Spirit's fire; do not treat prophecies with contempt" (v.19,20).

When the Spirit prompts you to do something, do it; do not hold back. I once heard of a man who said, "Sometimes when I think of how my wife works and blesses me, it's all I can do to keep from telling her that I love her"! There is a man being guided by the Spirit but he is putting the fire out. Do not do that. Go ahead and tell her you love her. You may have to pick her up from the floor afterward, but do not put out the Spirit's fire. I am as keen as anyone to stop Christianity becoming mere emotional. But I have no desire to see it become devoid of passion and feeling.

"Do not treat prophecies with contempt" (v.20). There seem to have been many prophets in the New Testament church. It is very understandable that God should have sent prophets to the church before the New Testament was available. At that time the word of God came to the church through apostles and through prophets, who were the living and infallible teachers of the church. Today, all of us have to acknowledge, the situation is very different. We have the word of God written down. So certainly there can be no apostle comparable to Peter, Paul or John. Equally certainly there are no prophets comparable to the biblical prophets. Otherwise we should have to add their words to Scripture the whole church would have to obey. In the primary sense in which these words are used in Scripture, there are no more such. Paul calls them the "foundation of the church" (Ephesians 2:20). The foundation is their teaching and that is finished. That really isn't controversial. The question is whether there are today some kinds of lesser gifts. Certainly God does give to some of his people a remarkable degree of insight, into Scripture, human nature and his particular will in specific situations. And perhaps it would be right to describe this insight as prophetic insight, or a prophetic gift.

Dr. F. F. Bruce writes, "The gift of prophesy – the declaration of the mind of God in the power of the Spirit." *(Word Biblical Commentary, 1 & 2 Thessalonians, F.F Bruce, Word Books, 1982).*

If the devil can't keep you from listening to the voice of God, he will try to push you too far. The apostle adds, "Test everything". Anyone can stand up and say in a deep tone of voice, "Thus says the Lord." We must learn to test what is said from what has already been revealed. Luke commended the Bereans for this, saying, "The Bereans were of more noble character than the Thessalonians, for they received the message with great eagerness and examined the scriptures every day to see if what Paul said was true" (Acts 17:11).

Don't become gullible, "Test everything. Hold on to the good. Avoid every kind of evil" (v.21,22).

Bruce says, "The use of God's gift of reason is a corrective to unrestrained enthusiasm. There is a saying widely ascribed to Jesus by writers in the early Christian centuries: 'Become approved moneychangers'. This was sometimes explained in terms of 1 Thessalonians 5:21,22. For example, Clement of Alexandria quotes it in the form: 'Become approved moneychangers, who reject much, but retain the good'. The distinguishing of genuine from counterfeit coinage is a good figure of speech for the distinguishing of true from false prophecy – or any other kind of religious teaching."

The thing the Lord seems to be asking me in response to Paul's admonition is, "Derek are you open and ready for new truth? Are you willing to keep on learning? There is so much you have not discovered." What can I say except, "I'm ready, Lord, keep me open to respond to what you guide but not to the whim the moment dictates".

Well, there you have the steps to 'getting it all together'. Under the guidance of the Holy Spirit. They are all intertwined. Dare to take an incisive inventory of your relationships with – Your Spiritual Leaders. With one Another. With God. Decide with God's help to act. Do it now.

CHAPTER 10   FOOTNOTE:
Living At Peace . . .
Turn that music off!

Here are some reflections on music. This information was considered helpful when presented at a Conference. I claim no originality.

Worship Wars

What significant change has occurred today more than any other in the western church? The answer in one word is - *music*. Today, what some call "worship wars," has removed 'peace' from many a church as they struggle with either pushing for change or resisting change that comes from utilising traditional worship music, as against what is often called contemporary worship music. Research reflects a serious culture change in western tastes for music, which naturally filters down into what Christians want in their worship of God in church services and what they want to listen to on radio.

Transition and Trends

Music in Church has always been in *"transition"* and changing. Check history and you discover some interesting trends –

4000 BC – harps and vertical flutes introduced in Egypt.

3000 BC – the bamboo pipe instrument invented in China.

2000 BC – trumpets in Denmark, percussion instruments added to Egyptian orchestras.

800 BC - five to seven tone scales added to traditional music in Babylon

550 BC – the diatonic scale invented for music in Greece.

50 BC – the oboe wind instrument appeared in Rome 500 AD – Peru used flutes, tubas and percussion instruments (drums).

1100 AD – bagpipes appeared in Scotland.

1325 AD – organ pedals invented for this instrument.

1465 AD – Printed music appeared in Europe.

1562 AD – Pope Pius IV banned the use of all instruments, except the organ as well as harmony singing and folk melodies from church services.

1565 AD – Women were banned from singing in churches.

1650 AD – Modern style harmony began to reappear in church worship.

1829 AD – the accordion was invented and used in the church.

1860 AD – Brass bands became popular in western culture.

1970 AD – popular praise and worship style of songs began in infancy

The evolution of music.

The point of all this is to show that music continuously evolves along with the varying culture of man, and probably will continue to do so as the years and centuries go by. As result of these and other factors of culture, the Christian Church and its music hymnals reflect many different styles of music. They all utilise a number of hymns, gospel songs and spirituals. Newer hymnals of the late 20th century began to also reflect the newest form of music we call today *"contemporary"* and *"praise"* music.

Why different styles?

Why do we have so many different styles of songs and singing in the Church? The answer is to be found in the relationship between songs and religious movements. The fact is every time religious people experience a new religious movement, we also experience the birth of a new musical style of singing to match that era of time and culture.

CHAPTER 11
Set Apart For God's Exclusive Use
1 Thessalonians 5: 23-27

A baby camel asked his mother, "Why do camels have large feet?" "That's easy", replied his mum. "It stops us sinking into the soft desert sand." "Mum why do we have lots of hair around our eyes?" "It's so that as we cross the desert and the wind blows, we don't get sand in our eyes." "Mum, why do camels have humps on our backs?" "That's easy", said his mother, "As we cross the desert, we might not find a water-hole for days on end, so we carry our own supply on tap." The question answered, the bay camel sat pensively for a few minutes before saying, "Mum, what on earth are we doing in London Zoo then?"

I know, I know, it not a true story. Of course not. But what about people falling short of their destiny in life? Most people today are pursuing one thing above all 'the good life'. Unfortunately, instead of the real thing we too often settle for a substitute. The great truth is that those who admit their selfishness and ask Jesus Christ to forgive them and become their Lord and Saviour, find a truth that sets them free to live with purpose. Don't idle away your time kicking dust in the human zoo. Admit the truth about yourself and reach out for the help that comes from the gospel.

189

Paul's closing blessing to the Thessalonians in 5:23-28 provides us a basis to function as the kind of human beings that God always intended us to be.

"May God himself, the God of peace, sanctify you through and through. May your whole spirit, soul and body be kept blameless at the coming of our Lord Jesus Christ. The one who calls you is faithful and he will do it. Brothers, pray for us. Greet all the brothers with a holy kiss. I charge you before the Lord to have this letter read to all the brothers".

The key is found in "God himself, the God of peace" (v.23). Peace is intrinsic to the character and existence of God. God is called "the God the peace" at least five other times in the New Testament (Romans 15:33;16:20; 2 Corinthians 13:11; Philippians 4:9; Hebrews 13:20). These citations explain that God's peace is more than the absence of conflict, it is more than tranquillity. It is completeness, soundness, welfare, wellbeing, wholeness. Invoking God as "the God of peace" is parallel to Jeremiah 29:11, which reads literally, "'For I know the plans I am planning for you, 'declares the Lord'." It is the nature of God to want to knit together what has become fragmented in us.

The truth for all of us who are his children is that our God is the "God of peace" and his plans for every one of us are for our wellbeing. None of his children are an exception nor ever will be. He desires to "sanctify you through and through" (v.23). Sanctify simply means "set apart for God's exclusive use."

There is – *Positional* sanctification (Hebrews 10:10); we have once and for all been set apart for God.

There is also *Practical* sanctification (2 Corinthians 7:1), a daily dealing with our sins and a growth in holiness.

All of this will culminate in *Perfect* sanctification (1 John 3:2), when we see Christ and become eternally like him. Expecting to see Jesus Christ is a great motivation for holy living.

What Paul seems to be praying is that the Thessalonians' entire spirits, souls and bodies be freely open, committed, receptive and utilised for the purpose of each parts' calling and that they all work in unity to accomplish the purpose of the total life of the Christian.

We are spirit, soul and body (v.23). God can touch you in all those areas. Our spirit, *pneuma*, is the most distinctive part of our nature. Unlike all other creatures, we have been given the capacity to know, communicate with and receive the Spirit of God. The blemished spirit of man, distorted by the fall, can be healed and recreated as a result of reconciliation through faith in Christ. Our spirit can be the post-resurrection home of the living Christ, the Holy Spirit. The soul, is the self-conscious seat of personality including intellect, emotion and will. Paul uses the Greek word *psuche* for our thinking, feeling, deciding capacities. The word is used extensively throughout the New Testament: 48 times as *soul,* 40 times as *life,* three times as *mind* and once as *heart.* I am convinced that Paul uses it in this Thessalonian passage very much as Moses does in Deuteronomy using *heart* for thought, emotion and will (see 6:5).

The inclusion of both spirit and soul was not a redundant coupling of synonyms. Paul wanted the Thessalonians to claim the capacity to know and receive God's Spirit, as well as become responsible in exercising their full intellectual, emotional and volitional potential as an expression of their faith.

Paul was also concerned about the physical health and purity of the body, *soma.* Our spirits and souls dwell in our bodies; and the Holy Spirit dwells in our spirits and utilises our souls to inspire our thoughts, engender our emotions and guide our wills. For Paul, the body is the temple of the Holy Spirit. He called for reverence and care of the body as holy, sacred, set apart to glorify God (see 1 Corinthians. 6:19,20). Paul longed for completeness in all facets of our nature; for our spirit, soul and body to march to the same drummer in harmony with God's will in all our life.

A question begs consideration: Why are there so few whole Christians? The reason is that many of us have resisted his invasion into all the aspects of our nature. It is possible to believe that Jesus is the Christ and still be a fragmented person. There are notional Christians whose faith has not entered emotion, will or body. Also there are emotional Christians who are willing to get their thinking straight as well as volitional Christians who are willing to do what's right without the power to do it. And there are others who need to discover how to express their faith in their physical lives. The body's habits, disabilities or passions must be brought under control of the Spirit.

Paul believed and lived in the assurance, "The one who calls you is faithful and he will do it" (v.24). The same faithfulness revealed in the Incarnation, the cross, Pentecost and Christ's presence would be expressed consistently in the growth of wholeness in the Thessalonians. They could count on it, says Paul. And so can we. Here is how he does it. He works continuously in our spirit, soul and body.

SPIRIT

Our spirit is the contact point with him. Since he is Spirit, he has made us capable of knowing him, experiencing his love and friendship. Our spirit is the control centre of the new life in Christ. Wholeness is begun when we yield our spirit to be filled with his Holy Spirit. Our first step to getting the right attitude to ourselves is to yield our spirits to his indwelling power and control.

SOUL

The next step is with our souls. Christ makes a beachhead in our spirit and then penetrates into our intellect, emotion and will. He captures our understanding, liberates our emotions and focuses our wills to do his will. To be whole in our soul is to surrender our minds to be the thinking agent of Christ. We must not avoid thinking through the deeper truth of the gospel in the sticky issues of life.

EMOTION

The same is true of our emotions. How we react emotionally in the present must be surrendered to the momentary guidance of the Spirit in our souls. There's no such thing as an unexpressed emotion. If our feelings are suppressed, they come out in some other way. God has created us with the capacity to feel. Emotional wholeness is bringing our feelings under the guidance of the mind of Christ. His mind in us sends the right signals into our emotions and helps us to respond as he would in any situation. We grow in emotional wholeness when we bring every feeling to him for his touch.

WILL

Closely related to our emotions is the will. This is our capacity to decide. We constantly face decisions for which we need his guidance. When he takes up residence in our spirits, his truth invades our minds and becomes the basis of our deciding. Truth must be obeyed if we are to be whole persons. Any truth, which is not acted on, actually becomes detrimental to further growth in wholeness. When an insight is not lived, it is worse than a chance lost; it works negatively to hinder future resolutions and implementation of thought.

BODY

The effective functioning of the body has a telling impact on our spirits and minds. A commitment to Christ includes care for our bodies. We are responsible as stewards of our physical health. Nutrition, exercise, rest and recreation are Christian disciplines as well as prayer, study and witnessing. The neglect of the body is a contradiction of our faith. Lack of rest and exercise can debilitate our discipleship. A physically exhausted Christian is an irritable tool for the Lord to use.

So Paul Concludes This Letter.

The three injunctions at the end of this letter are not particularly related. One is a personal prayer request, another emphasises the importance of demonstrating affection and love to each other. The third exhorted these believers to share the message of this letter with all the Christians in Thessalonica and the surrounding area.

"Brothers, pray for us" (v.25). Paul seldom focused on his own needs. However, he always acknowledged his need for prayer (Romans 15:30-32; 2 Corinthians 1:11; Ephesians 6:19,20; Philippians 1:19; Colossians 4:3,18; Psalm 22). Was the apostle trying to turn his request before God into a sure thing by such wide and persistent backing?

Steven Mosley has helpfully pointed out, "If we look at these appeals carefully, two things become evident: the involvement of those asked to pray and the confidence of the one asking."

The believers in Thessalonica were deeply bonded to Paul; they weren't praying for a stranger. They dated their spiritual birth to his testimony. They were also bound in ministry with Paul. They prayed as participants in the same movement; their hearts beat with his same passion.

Mosley concludes, "This leads us to suggest a guideline for making prayer more answerable: The more involved a petitioner is with the person or problem prayed for, the more significant his or her role as an intercessor before God. This does not mean, or course, that it is wrong to pray for strangers, but that we are most powerful in prayer when we don't pray from the sidelines."

The second element we can see in Paul's appeals for prayer is his cheery confidence. We don't find a man frantically gathering prayer support, like some candidate hustling votes at a political conventions, because he is so fearful of not getting what he asks for. On the contrary, the remarkable thing is that Paul seems to request prayer precisely because he is sure it will be answered in a certain way. The more people who pray, the more who will then be able to rejoice personally in the answer given. So, to make your requests more answerable, ask others to pray in a spirit of confidence, with a desire that they share in the happiness of the answer. You want those involved in some way in your life or in the matter you're praying for to turn their concern into specific petition.

Taking this a step further, Mosley illustrates, "During a weekly time of prayer, several missionaries began to talk about their present needs and make prayer requests. When Bob's turn came, his puffy cheeks, red eyes and constant use of a handkerchief made it obvious what he needed. 'I can't seem to shake this cold', he said quietly. 'It just keeps hanging on. I'd like you to pray that I'll be able to get rid of it' They all nodded politely, all except for the man's secretary, Lucille, a woman with soft grey hair and an angelic face. She said firmly, 'Sorry I'm not going to pray for you Bob'. The rest of the group looked at her in amazement. She continued, 'You've been staying at the office every night until ten with hardly a break for meals. You're working yourself to death. Now you want God to heal you. I don't think he will and I'm not going to pray about it.'

Lucille had such an impish look in her eyes as she spoke that the rest including Bob, couldn't help chuckling. The overworked man meekly promised to reform his lifestyle immediately and Lucille consented to pray".

If Bob's request had remained purely private, he could have much more easily gone on petitioning God for health and working himself to death. But fortunately there was another believer there to jolt him awake. One-to-one communication with God will always remain the heart and soul of prayer, but group petition serves as an important balancing element that sharpens our aim and keeps us on track of more answerable petitions… Selfish or wrong-headed prayers that are easy to repeat in private don't sound the same before fellow believers. We simply aim better when two or three are agreed on a certain petition. Openly talking about our goals creates more room in which wisdom can stake its claim". *(If Only God Would Answer, Steven Mosley, Navpress, 1992).*

Think about this for a moment. You are where you are today because somebody prayed for you. Somebody prayed and you came to Christ. Somebody prayed and you found a job. Somebody prayed and you were healed. Somebody prayed and you were rescued in the middle of the night. Somebody prayed and your marriage was saved. Somebody prayed and you didn't give up. Somebody prayed and you made the right decision. Somebody prayed and you experienced God's power. No one knows how much sin and sorrow we've been saved from because somebody prayed for us.

What is the application? Pray! Pray, pray, and keep on praying. Do for others what others have done for you. When we can serve people in no other way, we can pray for them. May God make us a praying people.

"Greet all the brothers with a holy kiss", adds Paul. 1Thessalonians 5:26 is one of five such exhortations in the New Testament (see Romans 16:16; 1 Corinthians 16:20; and also 2 Corinthians 13:12 and 1 Peter 5:14).

Justin Martyr (c. A.D. 150) suggests the exchange of the kiss is in the setting of Communion. It came after the prayers and before the bringing in of the bread and wine (1 Apol 65:2). The omission of the kiss of greeting even at an ordinary social meal was an occasion for remark (Luke 7:45); it was the more appropriate that it should feature in the meal where those in the fellowship of the church celebrated the one whose sacrifice had made them family. Perhaps Paul envisaged the letter being read at a Communion of the church – after the prayers, perhaps and just before the normal moment for the exchange kiss. This would not be an isolated instance among Paul's epistles: at the end of 1 Corinthians (16:20-22) the direction to "greet one another with a holy kiss" is followed by the quotation of some words from the communion service.

"If we may regard the closing verses of 1 Corinthians as a lead-in to the Lord's Supper, we can draw the conclusion that the Supper was introduced by the kiss of peace as a sign of living fellowship among the members. This was accompanied both by the pronouncement of a curse upon any who did not truly love the Lord and by the pronouncement of a blessing upon the Lord's people" *(Last Supper and Lord's Supper, I.H. Marshall, Paternoster Press, Exeter 1980).*

The important issue in this exhortation is not the form of greeting, but rather the meaning behind the greeting. The way in which people express care and affection varies from culture to culture. But whatever that greeting, it should always be a holy expression and meaningful.

Warren Wiersbe is on target when he writes, "I have been in churches where the congregation escaped like rats leaving a sinking ship. Fellowship is part of worship. The 'holy kiss' was not a sensual thing. Usually the men kissed the men, and the women kissed the women". *(Be Ready, Warren Wiersbe, Victor Books 1979).*

Let's not be so scared of the dangers of excesses that it becomes a phobia. I know men who touch their dog more than their children. Fellowship is part of worship. Christians, of all people, should be sincerely interested in one another and express that interest in a culturally acceptable way.

Paul ends with another reminder that the Word of God is the important thing in the local church. "I charge you before the Lord to have this letter read to all the brothers" (v.27). The sudden switch from the plural to the singular of the first person is significant. Probably Paul has taken the pen from his amanuensis to add the last words in his own hand (see also 2 Thessalonians 3:17). It's an extraordinary instruction. Already the Old Testament Scriptures were read in the public assembly, a custom taken over from the synagogue by the early Christian assemblies. But now the apostle says his letters are to be read in the public assembly as well! The clear implication is that he regarded the letter as on a par with the Old Testament Scriptures. Furthermore, he gives them no command to weigh or sift his teaching as in the case of those claiming to be prophets. No, they were to listen to everything the apostles wrote and they were to believe and obey it all. So clearly Paul puts his authority as an apostle above that of the prophets.

So today, even if there is some kind of subsidiary prophetic gift of insight, of far greater importance for the church is the teaching of the apostles, as it has been bequeathed to us in the New Testament and the public reading and exposition of the Scripture. It's that which edifies the church.

CHAPTER 12
Grace to You
1 Thessalonians 5:28

There are lines from literature and movies that become classics, remembered long after most are forgotten. One of those lines comes from the 1954 film *On the Waterfront* starring Marlon Brando. He plays a prize fighter named Terry Malloy. He is coerced by the crime mob to throw a fight he could easily have won. Sadly, the mob messenger is his brother, Charlie. His decision to lose begins a downward descent that ends his boxing career and keeps him in organised crime. Years later, Charlie tries to pressure Terry again. This time he is asked to give perjured testimony in court. They conversation goes back to the thrown boxing match years ago.

Charlie says, "You could have been another Billy Caan. That skunk we got or your manager, he brought you along too fast." Terry says, "It wasn't the manager. It was you, Charlie. You remember that night in the Garden you came down and said, "It's not your night, kid. It's not your night.' I could'a torn Wilson apart. I could'a had class! I couldn'a been a contender! I could'a been somebody!" One line summed up the deep regret of a lifetime: "I could'a been a contender!"

There are thousands of other stories that could be made into movies about regret. Most regrets are filed under the heading, "If I could live life over again." We take the L and E off of LIFE and leave ourselves with an IF. If our lives could be re-lived we might change the choices we have made.

Our English word "regret" partially comes from an old French word meaning "to weep." Regret is deep sorrow over which we return to tears constantly. Regret may be something we did or something we had done to us – either way the sorrow does not go away. Deep regrets are only in part about the moment of past decision. They cling to us because of their lasting consequences. Regrets are re-invigorated daily by the new pain that comes from yesterday's choices and consequences. Our lives are forever changed from what they could have been and should have been. There is no going back. But there is a way to go forward. Paul's closing words to 1 Thessalonians holds the key.

"The grace of the Lord Jesus Christ be with you"

When Thomas Carlyle was in the throes of composing his French Revolution, he wrote to his friend Emerson: "That beggarly Book hampers me every way. To fling it once for all into the fire were perhaps the best; yet I grudge to do that. It is impossible for you to figure what mood I am in. One sole thought. That Book! That weary Book occupies me continually. For the present, really, it is like a Nessus' shirt, burning you into madness; nay, it is also like a kind of panoply, rendering you invulnerable, insensible, to all other mischief's".

There stands the cost – the sweat and agony of being a dedicated spirit. Are you prepared for that – with Jesus? For he asks for nothing less. The stress of such involvement is immense. But it is worth it. For beyond it there is born the work produced by faith, labour prompted by love, endurance inspired by hope in our Lord Jesus Christ. And beyond that? God strengthens your hearts so that you will be blameless and holy in his presence when our Lord Jesus comes. No regrets.

But standing in front of a mirror saying, "I am determined to be all that my Lord wants me to be even if it kills me." It probably will. Take a look at Paul's final benediction. Here is the open secret.

Let's state it again, *"The grace of the Lord Jesus Christ be with you"* (v.28). A closing word of grace was the trademark of Paul in all his letters. "May God's unmerited, freely given favour rest on you".

What is grace?

Grace is God's action in our lives. G.R.A.C.E. - **G**od's **R**escuing **A**nd **C**aring Exertion. To the Corinthian Church Paul wrote, "I worked harder - yet not I, but the grace of God that was with me"

(1 Corinthians 15:10) Grace is God's exertion in our lives to help us. "As sin reigned in death, so also grace might reign through righteousness to bring eternal life through Jesus Christ our Lord." (Romans. 5:21). Grace is like a powerful ruler who exerts his control over us. "Whatever God has to say to us – and in all the New Testament letters there are things that search the heart and make it quake – begins and ends with grace …

All that God has been to man is summed up in Jesus Christ: all his gentleness and patience, all the holy passion of his love, is gathered up in grace. What more could one soul wish for another, that the grace of the Lord Jesus Christ should be with them?" *(James Denny, The Epistle to the Thessalonians, Hodder & Stoughton, 1892).*

Grace is the summary of God's blessings in Christ. I like to think of it as:

The A to Z of Blessings

I Am: **A**ccepted, **B**eloved, **C**hosen, **D**elivered, **E**nlightened and **F**orgiven.

I Have: **G**ifts, **H**ope, **I**nheritance, **J**ustification, **K**nowledge, **L**ove, **M**ercy, His **N**earness, **O**wnership, **P**eace and **Q**uickening of the Spirit.

205

I Am: **R**edeemed By His Blood,
               Sealed By The Spirit, **T**reasured,
               Understood and **V**alidated.

He gives His: **W**isdom and E**X**traordinary
               care, He is the **Y**es to the
               promises and the **Z**enith of it all
               will be that I live with him
               forever."

I like the saying chanted by a bunch of kids at an
American camp:

I may be black I may be brown,
I may be white I may be a clown, but -
I AM GOD'S CHILD.

I may be rich I may be poor,
I may wear a brace I may even snore, but -
I AM GOD'S CHILD.

I may be short I may be tall,
I may have hair I may be bald, but -
I AM GOD'S CHILD.

I may live in a house I may live in a trailer,
I may be successful I may be a failure, but -I
AM GOD'S CHILD.

I am a Sinner – but I'm also a Saint,
A nobody I certainly aint, because -
I AM GOD'S CHILD.

Have you received Christ's grace?

Say, "Here's my cup, Lord; fill it up, Lord." But please – don't get thrown off course by how God does it. He will put you in the place and with the people, which will tend most to develop spiritual graces. He puts one who is in a hurry with one who is slow; one who is quiet with one who is talkative. He puts one who is orderly with one who is untidy. He does this that both may learn lessons. Environment, you see, is often but an answer to prayer. We pray for perseverance. God sends those who tax us to the utmost. Why? "Suffering produces perseverance" (Romans 5:3). We pray for a greater reverent submission to our Lord. God sends suffering. Why? Because we learn obedience by the things we suffer (Hebrews 5:8). We pray for victory. Yet the things of this world sweep down upon us in a storm of temptations. Why? "This is the victory that has overcome the world, even our faith" (1 John 5:4). We pray for humility and strength. Some messenger of Satan torments us until we plead with God for its removal. Why? So we can learn that his strength is revealed in us by the realisation of our own weakness (2 Corinthians 12:10). We pray for union with Jesus. God severs natural ties and lets our best friends misunderstand or become indifferent to us. Why? That we may learn that "love is patient, love is kind . . . it keeps no record of wrongs . . . it always protects, always trusts, always hopes, always perseveres" (1 Corinthians 13:4-7). We ask to follow Jesus. He separates us from home and earthly security. Why? For he himself said, "Anyone of you who does not give up everything he has cannot be my disciple" (Luke 14:33).

So let us remember in the hard places, when things happen that we regret or cannot understand, that "Our Lord God Almighty reigns" (Revelation 19:6). What a release from petty worries. Bring your worry into the light of that great truth and just see how the fretting will fade and die. This is not hyperbole: it is proved experience and the grace of the Lord Jesus Christ is in it. The man who has his gaze riveted on the narrow little circle of his own experience, obsessed (like the poor creature in Bunyan's dream) with the sticks and straws and dust of the floor, never thinking of the stars and the crown, cannot see life in true perspective. Look away from all that. Take one long look into the face of the Lord God Almighty, even if it is five minutes in the morning to stabilise your soul by remembering Christ, how that would reinforce and liberate you! Yes! It is release – this great conviction – from the worries of life. "Hallelujah! For our Lord God Almighty reigns".

We are all afraid of something. Maybe you cross bridges before you get to them, you borrow imagined problems and expect the worst to happen. To be alive is to be afraid, because to be alive is to be in danger. Life is full of hazards. Life is full of risks. To be alive is to be vulnerable to life's contingencies. Just when we think we're safest, they happen.

Some fears are necessary and productive. In Moby Dick, Starbuck the first mate, says, "I will have no man on my boat who is not afraid of a whale." To be brave is to be scared. I hope that when we drive cars we have a certain fear. I hope that teachers and parents, counsellors and pastors and anyone who works with people, tremble with the responsibility of the care of human lives. I hope that we at Good News Broadcasting are awestruck at the responsibility we have in spreading the Word of God.

But some people become so desperately afraid and worried that life turns into a nightmare. Fear and anxiety can become dangerous. Fear and worry can render us irrational, can lead to erratic thinking, distort reality, can inhibit and frustrate us and leave us deficient and totally paralysed. Charles Spurgeon once said, "Anxiety does not empty tomorrow of its sorrow - only today of its strength."

Jesus wants to teach us, "Do not be anxious about tomorrow. Tomorrow will take care of itself." Jesus teaches us, "Do not be afraid," which in the Greek of the Gospels translates as, "do not be ruled or tyrannised or immobilised by fear."

Inner peace comes when we are not afraid of life because we come to know that there is nothing in life that can destroy who we are as a child of God. He loves us with a perfect love that never ends. All of our fears pale in comparison to the love with which God loves us and the love we may have with which we love one another. Nothing compares. Nothing can overcome that love. Not even death.

Throughout the Gospels Jesus teaches us to be worth what we are. Believe the best about yourself and behold the miracle of it coming true. Rejoice at your God-given place in the sun. No one is excluded - not one. You are not excluded from that! Within you there is divine possibility, no matter how you disbelieve it, despair of it or distort it. That is because of grace.

While we may make mistakes, we are not a mistake; while we may fail, we are not a failure; while we may lose, we are not a loser; while we create our own problems and get tangled up in the contradictions of life, we are never a problem; while we may have weaknesses and be different from most others, we are not weak and defective; while we may have a handicapping condition, we are never a handicap; while we may choose wrongly and turn from our best and even from God, a sinner is never all we are. We are always much, much more because we are a child of God. The angels sang the day we were born because we too, are a child of God.

Let us rise up and praise him, for he is answering. May we hold high before us the miracle of being filled with his grace. There is more grace for our lives as we open our lives more fully to him. Open the door to his grace in your life. He will begin to make you whole. No regrets.

About – 'Facing A New Day...

Using **1 Thessalonians,** Dr. Derek Stringer unlocks the secrets of Christian living and growth. Here is information which leads to transformation. Discover how to change for the better as Dr. Stringer combines textual interpretation with up-to-date illustrations from contemporary life.

Dr. Stringer is the National Director of Good News Broadcasting Association (UK). He also travels internationally preaching and teaching, and is a visiting lecturer at Bible Schools. He is the radio voice for GNBA (UK). Derek's popular Bible Teaching Programmes can be heard on Premier Christian Radio. He also writes devotional Bible messages for the GNBA bi-monthly e-mail as well as answering the difficult questions asked by the radio listeners. Further details of Derek and his ministry can be found on the GNBA web site. He can be contacted through the GNBA Office at Ranskill. If you wish to be added to the GNBA mailing list, you should also contact the Ranskill office, or visit the web site. Both are detailed below.

Good News Broadcasting Association (UK)
Ranskill. DN22 8NN. England
Email:info@gnba.net   Web site:www.gnba.net